# The South Asian Association for Regional Cooperation (SAARC)

The South Asian Association for Regional Cooperation (SAARC) is an international organization comprised of the eight countries in South Asia. This work aims to examine the institutional structure, objectives and effectiveness of SAARC in its role as South Asia's leading regional institution.

Drawing on original research it offers a fresh and accessible account of SAARC, arguing that South Asia forms a unique regional security complex that enables certain forms of regional cooperation and bars cooperation on other issue areas.

The text provides a comprehensive introduction to SAARC, describing the historical developments that led to its formation and examining key issues such as:

- the inner workings of regional centers and their success in implementing the decisions reached at SAARC summits;
- how SAARC has sought to address critical new security challenges, such as health pandemics, terrorism, and energy security;
- South Asia's economic cooperation and the South Asia Free Trade Agreement (SAFTA);
- challenges that expansion poses to the organization, particularly China's suggestion to expand beyond the traditional borders of South Asia.

The work aims to evaluate what scope there is for formal institutions like SAARC to provide a permanent regional security architecture within which South Asian countries can effectively address important issues, and will be of great interest to all students and scholars of Asian security studies and institutions in general and students and scholars of international relations in South Asia in particular.

**Lawrence Sáez** is Senior Lecturer in Comparative and International Politics in the Department of Politics and International Studies at the School of Oriental and African Studies (SOAS) where he is also Director of the Center of South Asian Studies.

## Routledge Global Institutions

Edited by Thomas G. Weiss
The CUNY Graduate Center, New York, USA
and Rorden Wilkinson
University of Manchester, UK

## About the series

The Global Institutions Series is designed to provide readers with comprehensive, accessible, and informative guides to the history, structure, and activities of key international organizations as well as books that deal with topics of key importance in contemporary global governance. Every volume stands on its own as a thorough and insightful treatment of a particular topic, but the series as a whole contributes to a coherent and complementary portrait of the phenomenon of global institutions at the dawn of the millennium.

Books are written by recognized experts, conform to a similar structure, and cover a range of themes and debates common to the series. These areas of shared concern include the general purpose and rationale for organizations, developments over time, membership, structure, decision-making procedures, and key functions. Moreover, current debates are placed in historical perspective alongside informed analysis and critique. Each book also contains an annotated bibliography and guide to electronic information as well as any annexes appropriate to the subject matter at hand.

The volumes currently published are:

**56 The South Asian Association for Regional Cooperation (2011)**
An emerging collaboration architecture
*by Lawrence Sáez (University of London)*

**55 The UN Human Rights Council (2011)**
*by Bertrand G. Ramcharan (Geneva Graduate Institute of International and Development Studies)*

**54 The Responsibility to Protect (2011)**
Cultural perspectives in the Global South
*edited by Rama Mani (University of Oxford) and Thomas G. Weiss (The CUNY Graduate Center)*

53 **The International Trade Center (2011)**
Promoting exports for development
*by Stephen Browne (FUNDS Project) and Sam Laird (University of Nottingham)*

52 **The Idea of World Government (2011)**
From ancient times to the twenty-first century
*by James A. Yunker (Western Illinois University)*

51 **Humanitarianism Contested (2011)**
Where angels fear to tread
*by Michael Barnett (George Washington University) and Thomas G. Weiss (The CUNY Graduate Center)*

50 **The Organization of American States (2011)**
Global governance away from the media
*by Monica Herz (Institute of International Relations, Catholic University, Rio de Janeiro)*

49 **Non-Governmental Organizations in World Politics (2011)**
The construction of global governance
*by Peter Willetts (City University, London)*

48 **The Forum on China-Africa Cooperation (FOCAC) (2011)**
*by Ian Taylor (University of St. Andrews)*

47 **Global Think Tanks (2011)**
Policy networks and governance
*by James G. McGann (University of Pennsylvania) with Richard Sabatini*

46 **United Nations Educational, Scientific and Cultural Organization (UNESCO) (2011)**
Creating norms for a complex world
*by J.P. Singh (Georgetown University)*

45 **The International Labour Organization (2011)**
Coming in from the cold
*by Steve Hughes (Newcastle University) and Nigel Haworth (University of Auckland)*

44 **Global Poverty (2010)**
How global governance is failing the poor
*by David Hulme (University of Manchester)*

43 **Global Governance, Poverty, and Inequality (2010)**
*edited by Jennifer Clapp (University of Waterloo) and Rorden Wilkinson (University of Manchester)*

42 **Multilateral Counter-Terrorism (2010)**
The global politics of cooperation and contestation
*by Peter Romaniuk (John Jay College of Criminal Justice, CUNY)*

41 **Governing Climate Change (2010)**
*by Peter Newell (University of East Anglia) and Harriet A. Bulkeley (Durham University)*

40 **The UN Secretary-General and Secretariat (2nd edition, 2010)**
*by Leon Gordenker (Princeton University)*

39 **Preventive Human Rights Strategies (2010)**
*by Bertrand G. Ramcharan (Geneva Graduate Institute of International and Development Studies)*

38 **African Economic Institutions (2010)**
*by Kwame Akonor (Seton Hall University)*

37 **Global Institutions and the HIV/AIDS Epidemic (2010)**
Responding to an international crisis
*by Franklyn Lisk (University of Warwick)*

36 **Regional Security (2010)**
The Capacity of International Organizations
*by Rodrigo Tavares (United Nations University)*

35 **The Organisation for Economic Co-operation and Development (2009)**
*by Richard Woodward (University of Hull)*

34 **Transnational Organized Crime (2009)**
*by Frank Madsen (University of Cambridge)*

33 **The United Nations and Human Rights (2nd edition, 2009)**
A guide for a new era
*by Julie A. Mertus (American University)*

32 **The International Organization for Standardization (2009)**
Global governance through voluntary consensus
*by Craig N. Murphy (Wellesley College) and JoAnne Yates (Massachusetts Institute of Technology)*

31 **Shaping the Humanitarian World (2009)**
*by Peter Walker (Tufts University) and Daniel G. Maxwell (Tufts University)*

30 **Global Food and Agricultural Institutions (2009)**
*by John Shaw*

**29 Institutions of the Global South (2009)**
*by Jacqueline Anne Braveboy-Wagner (City College of New York, CUNY)*

**28 International Judicial Institutions (2009)**
The architecture of international justice at home and abroad
*by Richard J. Goldstone (Retired Justice of the Constitutional Court of South Africa) and Adam M. Smith (Harvard University)*

**27 The International Olympic Committee (2009)**
The governance of the Olympic system
*by Jean-Loup Chappelet (IDHEAP Swiss Graduate School of Public Administration) and Brenda Kübler-Mabbott*

**26 The World Health Organization (2009)**
*by Kelley Lee (London School of Hygiene and Tropical Medicine)*

**25 Internet Governance (2009)**
The new frontier of global institutions
*by John Mathiason (Syracuse University)*

**24 Institutions of the Asia-Pacific (2009)**
ASEAN, APEC, and beyond
*by Mark Beeson (University of Birmingham)*

**23 UNHCR (2008)**
The politics and practice of refugee protection into the twenty-first century
*by Gil Loescher (University of Oxford), Alexander Betts (University of Oxford), and James Milner (University of Toronto)*

**22 Contemporary Human Rights Ideas (2008)**
*by Bertrand G. Ramcharan (Geneva Graduate Institute of International and Development Studies)*

**21 The World Bank (2008)**
From reconstruction to development to equity
*by Katherine Marshall (Georgetown University)*

**20 The European Union (2008)**
*by Clive Archer (Manchester Metropolitan University)*

**19 The African Union (2008)**
Challenges of globalization, security and governance
*by Samuel M. Makinda (Murdoch University) and F. Wafula Okumu (McMaster University)*

**18 Commonwealth (2008)**
Inter- and non-state contributions to global governance
*by Timothy M. Shaw (Royal Roads University)*

**17 The World Trade Organization (2007)**
Law, economics, and politics
*by Bernard M. Hoekman (World Bank) and Petros C. Mavroidis (Columbia University)*

**16 A Crisis of Global Institutions? (2007)**
Multilateralism and international security
*by Edward Newman (University of Birmingham)*

**15 UN Conference on Trade and Development (2007)**
*by Ian Taylor (University of St. Andrews) and Karen Smith (University of Stellenbosch)*

**14 The Organization for Security and Co-operation in Europe (2007)**
*by David J. Galbreath (University of Aberdeen)*

**13 The International Committee of the Red Cross (2007)**
A neutral humanitarian actor
*by David P. Forsythe (University of Nebraska) and Barbara Ann Rieffer-Flanagan (Central Washington University)*

**12 The World Economic Forum (2007)**
A multi-stakeholder approach to global governance
*by Geoffrey Allen Pigman (Bennington College)*

**11 The Group of 7/8 (2007)**
*by Hugo Dobson (University of Sheffield)*

**10 The International Monetary Fund (2007)**
Politics of conditional lending
*by James Raymond Vreeland (Georgetown University)*

**9 The North Atlantic Treaty Organization (2007)**
The enduring alliance
*by Julian Lindley-French (Center for Applied Policy, University of Munich)*

**8 The World Intellectual Property Organization (2006)**
Resurgence and the development agenda
*by Chris May (University of the West of England)*

**7 The UN Security Council (2006)**
Practice and promise
*by Edward C. Luck (Columbia University)*

6 **Global Environmental Institutions (2006)**
*by Elizabeth R. DeSombre (Wellesley College)*

5 **Internal Displacement (2006)**
Conceptualization and its consequences
*by Thomas G. Weiss (The CUNY Graduate Center) and David A. Korn*

4 **The UN General Assembly (2005)**
*by M. J. Peterson (University of Massachusetts, Amherst)*

3 **United Nations Global Conferences (2005)**
*by Michael G. Schechter (Michigan State University)*

2 **The UN Secretary-General and Secretariat (2005)**
*by Leon Gordenker (Princeton University)*

1 **The United Nations and Human Rights (2005)**
A guide for a new era
*by Julie A. Mertus (American University)*

Books currently under contract include:

**The Regional Development Banks**
Lending with a regional flavor
*by Jonathan R. Strand (University of Nevada)*

**Millennium Development Goals (MDGs)**
For a people-centered development agenda?
*by Sakiko Fukada-Parr (The New School)*

**Peacebuilding**
From concept to commission
*by Robert Jenkins (The CUNY Graduate Center)*

**Human Security**
*by Don Hubert (University of Ottawa)*

**UNICEF**
*by Richard Jolly (University of Sussex)*

**FIFA**
*by Alan Tomlinson (University of Brighton)*

**International Law, International Relations, and Global Governance**
*by Charlotte Ku (University of Illinois)*

**The Bank for International Settlements**
The politics of global financial supervision in the age of high finance
*by Kevin Ozgercin (SUNY College at Old Westbury)*

**International Migration**
*by Khalid Koser (Geneva Center for Security Policy)*

**Global Health Governance**
*by Sophie Harman (City University, London)*

**The Council of Europe**
*by Martyn Bond (University of London)*

**Human Development**
*by Richard Ponzio*

**The United Nations Development Programme and System**
*by Stephen Browne (FUNDS Project)*

**Religious Institutions and Global Politics**
*by Katherine Marshall (Georgetown University)*

**The Group of Twenty (G20)**
*by Andrew F. Cooper (Center for International Governance Innovation, Ontario) and Ramesh Thakur (Balsillie School of International Affairs, Ontario)*

**The International Monetary Fund (2nd edition)**
Politics of conditional lending
*by James Raymond Vreeland (Georgetown University)*

**The UN Global Compact**
*by Catia Gregoratti (Lund University)*

**Security Governance in Regional Organizations**
*Edited by Emil Kirchner (University of Essex) and Roberto Dominguez (Suffolk University)*

**UN Institutions for Women's Rights**
*by Charlotte Patton (York College, CUNY) and Carolyn Stephenson (University of Hawaii)*

**International Aid**
*by Paul Mosley (University of Sheffield)*

**Maritime Piracy**
*by Bob Haywood and Roberta Spivak*

For further information regarding the series, please contact:

Craig Fowlie, Publisher, Politics & International Studies
Taylor & Francis
2 Park Square, Milton Park, Abingdon
Oxford OX14 4RN, UK
+44 (0)207 842 2057 Tel
+44 (0)207 842 2302 Fax
Craig.Fowlie@tandf.co.uk
www.routledge.com

# The South Asian Association for Regional Cooperation (SAARC)

## An emerging collaboration architecture

**Lawrence Sáez**

Routledge
Taylor & Francis Group
LONDON AND NEW YORK

First published 2011
by Routledge
2 Park Square, Milton Park, Abingdon, Oxon, OX14 4RN

Simultaneously published in the USA and Canada
by Routledge
270 Madison Avenue, New York, NY 10016

*Routledge is an imprint of the Taylor & Francis Group, an informa business*



*British Library Cataloguing in Publication Data*
A catalogue record for this book is available from the British Library

*Library of Congress Cataloging in Publication Data*
Sáez, Lawrence, 1965–
The South Asian Association for Regional Cooperation (SAARC): an emerging collaboration architecture / Lawrence Sáez.
p. cm. – (Global institutions)
Includes bibliographical references and index.
1. South Asian Association for Regional Cooperation. 2. South Asia–Foreign relations. 3. South Asian cooperation. 4. Interregionalism–South Asia. I. Title.
DS341.S235 2011
327.54–dc22
2011001229

ISBN 13: 978-0-415-57628-4 (hbk)
ISBN 13: 978-0-203-80880-1 (ebk)

Typeset in Times New Roman by
Taylor & Francis Books

# Contents

# Illustrations

## Tables



## Figures

## Boxes

# Foreword

The current volume is the fifty-sixth title in a dynamic series on global institutions. These books provide readers with definitive guides to the most visible aspects of what many of us know as "global governance." Remarkable as it may seem, there exist relatively few books that offer in-depth treatments of prominent global bodies, processes, and associated issues, much less an entire series of concise and complementary volumes. Those that do exist are either out of date, inaccessible to the non-specialist reader, or seek to develop a specialized understanding of particular aspects of an institution or process rather than offer an overall account of its functioning and situate it within the increasingly dense global institutional network. Similarly, existing books have often been written in highly technical language or have been crafted "in-house" and are notoriously self-serving and narrow.

The advent of electronic media has undoubtedly helped research and teaching by making data and primary documents of international organizations more widely available, but it has complicated matters as well. The growing reliance on the Internet and other electronic methods of finding information about key international organizations and processes has served, ironically, to limit the educational and analytical materials to which most readers have ready access—namely, books. Public relations documents, raw data, and loosely refereed websites do not make for intelligent analysis. Official publications compete with a vast amount of electronically available information, much of which is suspect because of its ideological or self-promoting slant. Paradoxically, a growing range of purportedly independent websites offering analyses of the activities of particular organizations has emerged, but one inadvertent consequence has been to frustrate access to basic, authoritative, readable, critical, and well-researched texts. The market for such has actually been reduced by the ready availability of varying quality electronic materials.

For those of us who teach, research, and operate in the area, such restricted access to information and analyses has been frustrating. We were delighted when Routledge saw the value of a series that bucks this trend and provides key reference points to the most significant global institutions and issues. They are betting that serious students and professionals will want serious analyses. We have assembled a first-rate team of authors to address that market. Our intention is to provide one-stop shopping for all readers—students (both undergraduate and postgraduate), negotiators, diplomats, practitioners from nongovernmental and intergovernmental organizations, and interested parties alike—seeking insights into the most prominent institutional aspects of global governance.

## SAARC

Despite the rekindling of a modicum of interest in South Asia by academics and policymakers scrambling to make sense of the "emergence"[1] of the BICs[2] (Brazil, India, China) and the "Next 11,"[3] South Asia has attracted surprisingly little attention in the international relations literature broadly and almost no work of note dealing with its institutions.[4] Scholarly and lay interest was piqued momentarily by India and Pakistan's nuclear declarations and continuing hostility; Sri Lanka's civil war; the plight of Nobel laureate Aun San Suu Kyi and the military junta in Burma; the Maldives' impending submersion under the Indian Ocean through sea level rise; periodic natural catastrophes in Bangladesh; the massacre of the Nepalese royal family; and the "discovery"of wild tigers living in Bhutan's mountains. But these are exceptions in a general pattern of neglect. Indeed, the only time South Asia gets any real academic attention results from a focus on radical Islamism and terrorism in Pakistan and Afghanistan or Indonesia. Even then, however, analyses are seldom "about" these places but are instead about the US-led war on terror.

It is precisely because more than one-fifth of the world's population lives in the eight countries that comprise South Asia (Bangladesh, Bhutan, Pakistan, India, the Maldives, Sri Lanka, Nepal, and Burma) that an exploration of its principal institution—the South Asian Association for Regional Cooperation, SAARC—is conspicuous by its absence. There are, however, other compelling reasons for bringing SAARC to the fore. It manages to provide an institutional framework in which two of the world's most determined rivals, India and Pakistan, work together. Likewise, SAARC associates with other countries that have histories of vexed relations. Moreover, South Asia's immediate neighbors add into the mix tensions between India and China and a competition for influence in the Indian Ocean region. Indeed, given these it is quite a wonder that South Asia is not at the forefront of the study of international relations and SAARC a staple of classes on international organization.

We were delighted then when Lawrence Sáez approached us. Not only is the topic compelling, he is a leading light in the field of South Asia studies and knows his way around SAARC. He is a Senior Lecturer in Comparative and International Politics, and Director of the Center of South Asian Studies, at the School of Oriental and African Studies (SOAS), University of London; and an Associate Fellow in the International Economics program at Chatham House. He has written extensively on the area including *Federalism without a Center: The Impact of Political Reform and Economic Liberalization on India's Federal System* (2002), *Banking Reform in India and China* (2004), and *Coalition Politics and Hindu Nationalism* (2005).[5]

We are delighted to have this book in the series and to include Lawrence in our stable of authors; a nice complement to other volumes in the series on Africa, Europe, and the Americas.[6] His book offers a comprehensive and concise overview of and insight into SAARC, which enriches the literature on global institutions. We wholeheartedly recommend it to our readers. As always, we welcome comments from our readers.

Thomas G. Weiss, The CUNY Graduate Center, New York, USA
Rorden Wilkinson, University of Manchester, UK
February 2011

# Acknowledgements

My interest in SAARC originated over 25 years ago, while I was an undergraduate exchange student at Hindu College, University of Delhi. I distinctly remember sitting on a sunny December afternoon in Kamala park in Bhopal, facing the lower lake. My friend, Mark Johnson, who was an avid reader of Indian newspapers, commented cynically on the creation of a new regional organization, initially called the South Asia Regional Cooperation. In Mark Johnson's initial assessment, SARC would be a complete waste of time and money. To be fair, many subsequent evaluations of SAARC have some similarly minded views of the association. This book, however, is not a hatchet job of SAARC, pointing out its many inadequacies. Within the limits of my capacity to obtain publicly accessible material, I have tried to offer a balanced view of SAARC's failures and achievements. I have also attempted to present SAARC within the context of larger theoretical debates, particularly in the international relations literature, on optimal institutional design and institutional capabilities.

Although my name appears on the cover, every author knows that writing a book is never a one-person show. I would like to thank a number of individuals without whose help this project would not have been made possible in its current form. First and foremost, I would like to thank Stuti Kochhar, Sarah Holz, Zaad Mahmood, Vinitha Revi, and Jessica Steinemann for providing useful preparatory research assistance along various stages of this project. I would also like to thank Nicola Parkin, Alison Phillips, Thomas Weiss, and Rorden Wilkinson.

I conducted fieldwork research at the SAARC Secretariat in Kathmandu and at various regional centers. I would like to thank the SAARC secretary general, Sheel Kant Sharma, and the senior personal assistant to the SAARC secretary general, Kumar Shrestra, for enabling me to meet with directors of the secretariat's Working Divisions. My meetings with SAARC secretariat staff (at all levels) were extremely informative and were carried out with a high level of openness. Nevertheless, as I promised my interlocutors during my informal meetings, private opinions or observations about the SAARC Secretariat have not been attributed to any single individual. The librarians at the SAARC Documentation Center in New Delhi were extremely helpful, so I would like to thank Bhavesh Patel. I would also like to thank scholars and practitioners who provided guidance and clarification on key facets of the work. In particular, I would like to thank Monika Barthwal-Datta and Arif Zaman.

I give special thanks to my ever patient wife, Joy, for providing support during critical stages of my field work. This book is dedicated to my mother, Elena Vargas, who died from a brain hemorrhage in January 2009.

# Abbreviations and acronyms

| | |
|---|---|
| ADB | Asian Development Bank |
| ADPC | Asian Disaster Preparedness Center |
| AJK | Azaad Jammu o-Kashmir |
| AMDISA | Association of Management and Development Institutions in South Asia |
| APT | Asia Pacific Telecommunity |
| ASEAN | Association of South East Asian Nations |
| AU | African Union |
| BIISS | Bangladesh Institute of International and Strategic Studies |
| CASS | Chinese Academy of Social Sciences |
| CBMs | Confidence-building measures |
| CCPIT | China Council for the Promotion of International Trade |
| CEC | Committee on Economic Cooperation |
| CENTCOM | US Central Command |
| CIDA | Canadian International Development Agency |
| CIRDAP | Center on Integrated Rural Development for Asia and the Pacific |
| CSTO | Collective Security Treaty Organization |
| CTBT | Comprehensive Test Ban Treaty |
| ECO | Economic Cooperation Organization |
| EPZ | Export Processing Zone |
| EU | European Union |
| FAO | Food and Agriculture Organization |
| FAPSS | Federation of Association of Pediatric Surgeons of SAARC Countries |
| FSIO | Federation of State Insurance Organizations of SAARC Countries |
| GSP | Generalized System of Preferences |

| | |
|---|---|
| GTZ | Deutsche Gesellschaft für Technische Zusammenarbeit |
| HIMAWANTI | Hindukush Himalayan Grassroots Women's Natural Resources Management |
| IAK | Indian-administered Kashmir |
| IDA | International Development Association |
| IGG | Inter-governmental Group |
| IGEG | Inter-governmental Expert Group |
| IOK | Indian-occupied Kashmir |
| IPA | Integrated program of action |
| ISIC | International Standard Industrial Classification |
| ISO | International Standards Organization |
| ITU | International Telecommunications Union |
| JSF | Japan Special Fund |
| LOC | Line of Control |
| MDGs | Millennium Development Goals |
| MERCOSUR | Mercado Común del Sur |
| NATO | North Atlantic Treaty Organization |
| NGO | Non-governmental Organization |
| NNPT | Nuclear Non-proliferation Treaty |
| OAU | Organization of African Unity |
| PAK | Pakistan-administered Kashmir |
| POK | Pakistan-occupied Kashmir |
| PPP | Purchasing power parity |
| PTB | Physikalisch-Technische Bundesanstalt |
| RCD | Regional Cooperation for Development |
| RSSC | Radiological Society of SAARC Countries |
| SAARC | South Asian Association for Regional Cooperation |
| SAARCFUW | SAARC Federation of University Women |
| SAARCH | South Asian Association for Regional Cooperation of Architects |
| SAARCLAW | South Asian Association for Regional Co-operation in Law |
| SACEP | South Asia Cooperative Environment Program |
| SACODiL | SAARC Consortium on Open and Distance Learning |
| SADF | South Asian Development Fund |
| SAFA | South Asian Federation of Accountants |
| SAFE | South Asian Federation of Exchanges |
| SAFMA | South Asian Free Media Association |
| SAFTA | South Asian Free Trade Area |
| SAIC | SAARC Agricultural Information Center |
| SAPTA | SAARC Preferential Trading Agreement |

| | |
|---|---|
| SARAD | South Asian Regional Association of Dermatologists, Venereologists and Leprologists |
| SARC | South Asian Regional Cooperation |
| SARSO | SAARC Regional Standards Organisation |
| SCCI | SAARC Chambers of Commerce and Industry |
| SCO | Shanghai Cooperation Organization |
| SDEF | SAARC Diploma Engineers Forum |
| SFO | SAARC Federation of Oncologists |
| SGIB | SAARC Gender Info Base |
| SSCS | SAARC Surgical Care Society |
| STF | SAARC Teachers Federation |
| STOMD | SAARC Terrorist Offences Monitoring Desk |
| SWA | SAARC Women's Association in Sri Lanka |
| UNAIDS | Joint United Nations Programme on HIV/AIDS |
| UNCTAD | United Nations Conference on Trade and Development |
| UNDP | United Nations Development Program |
| UNEP | United Nations Environment Program |
| UNESCAP | United Nations Economic and Social Commission Program |
| UNESCO | United Nations Educational, Scientific and Cultural Organization |
| UNICEF | United Nations Children's Fund |
| UNIDO | United Nations Industrial Development Organization |
| UNIFEM | United Nations Development Fund for Women |
| UN/ISDR | United Nations International Strategy for Disaster Reduction |
| UNODC | United Nations Office on Drugs and Crime |
| UNPF | United Nations Population Fund |
| WHO | World Health Organization |

# Introduction

The South Asian Association for Regional Cooperation (SAARC) is the most important regional economic and political institution binding the countries of South Asia. For a variety of overlapping historical antecedents, the precise delimitation of South Asia as a region is not always clear, but generally incorporates the contiguous geographic boundaries extending from modern-day Afghanistan through Myanmar (Burma), including the countries based in the Indian subcontinent. SAARC was formally founded in 1985 when the heads of state of seven countries in South Asia (namely Bangladesh, Bhutan, India, the Maldives, Nepal, Pakistan and Sri Lanka) held an inaugural summit in Dhaka, Bangladesh. Since its inception, SAARC has served as an important forum for institutional links among South Asian countries. At the time of SAARC's creation, though, South Asia was experiencing a great deal of turmoil. For instance, India was beset by a host of challenging internal security issues in the Punjab and along its northeastern provinces, an area of traditional ethnic unrest. Pakistan was a front-line state in a covert war in Afghanistan on account of the Soviet Union's invasion of that country. Likewise, Sri Lanka's civil war was getting underway. In light of these circumstances, the creation of a regional institution to enhance multilateral cooperation was seen as a welcome antidote to the internal realities then facing these countries.

Despite the gradual emergence of South Asia as an important focal point for global economic activity, SAARC has not attracted a great deal of scholarly interest. Moreover, much of the extant work has not reached an audience beyond South Asia, primarily because there has been a tendency toward insularity among scholars writing about South Asia and its institutions. The existing insularity of the study of SAARC divorces it from the study of other international organizations. In addition, this type of intellectual insularity has had a dampening effect on the development of comparative research designs that would invariably highlight lessons that other institutions may have for overcoming the inevitable structural obstacles that are present in all multilateral institutions. As a result, there is very little solid academic work comparing SAARC to other similar regional institutions. For instance, there are merely a handful of books which discuss SAARC's relations with the European Union (EU), while others draw some comparisons vis-à-vis the Association of South East Asian Nations (ASEAN), largely focusing on issues of regional integration.[1] There is, rather surprisingly, almost no scholarly work comparing SAARC with the African Union (AU), the Shanghai Cooperation Organization (SCO), or the Mercado Común del Sur (MERCOSUR).[2]

In addition, one must approach a study of SAARC with some trepidation, as it is easy to get swamped in the association's apparent complexity. Although SAARC has not been perceived as a particularly effective regional institution, it has generated a seemingly endless supply of initiatives, summit declarations, communiqués, and expert committee reports. Similarly, although it is relatively small in size, SAARC has sponsored a large number of ancillary institutions, which in turn have produced a vast number of policy reports and the like. Erring on the side of providing a comprehensive understanding of SAARC, another discouraging feature of previous books about SAARC has been that they have tended to be atheoretical and have instead emphasized narrative summaries of the internal mechanisms of SAARC and the association's summits. For instance, one of the more lucid works about SAARC, O. P. Goel's two-volume *India and SAARC Engagements* provides an exhaustive description about the declarations emerging from the first 10 SAARC summits.[3] Likewise, Dhirendra Dwivedi's *SAARC: Problems and Prospects* builds on a similar premise that focuses on the outcome of summits, in this particular case providing a narrative description of the first 12 SAARC summits.[4] Although these declarations offer important objectives of the association, books focusing on summit declarations could be perceived as being excessively narrow and descriptive. They also could provide a misleading interpretation that the stated purpose in a summit declaration necessarily translates into action. Overall, there is no reason to downplay the important contribution of these studies. However, the problem with the current state of the research on SAARC is that the insights that it generates are not easily generalizable and thus do not contribute as much to our cumulative understanding of regional institutions as one would wish.

Over time, interest in SAARC has also spilled over to the policy field and as such the institution has grown numerically. For instance, in November 2005, Afghanistan was added as the eighth formal member of SAARC. Other countries (Australia, China, Iran, Japan, Mauritius, Myanmar, South Korea, and the United States) and intergovernmental institutions (the European Union) currently enjoy observer status. Some of these countries have mulled over the idea of seeking formal membership to SAARC, though extending club rights to other countries outside of those that are already members has generated some opposition.

The analysis of regional institutions like SAARC poses a number of challenges. The literature on optimal institutional design, for instance, provides a possible avenue from which to evaluate the prospects of success of institutions like SAARC. A key feature of the theoretical literature on regional integration has focused on the difficulty of integration in situations where one component unit enjoys a disproportionate share of economic or military power. In the case of SAARC, India enjoys a disproportionate share of economic and military power in the region. In 1985, the year of the creation of SAARC, India's share of regional GDP was 73 percent. In 2008, India's share of regional GDP had grown to 79 percent.[5] India also has a distinct advantage over its neighbors in terms of total armed forces. Nearly 60 percent of the active duty armed forces in South Asia are from India.[6] India also outspends its neighbors in terms of military expenditure: more than 80 percent of the total in South Asia.[7] India also dominates South Asia in terms of population size. Nearly 75 percent of the population of South Asia lives in India. Viewed from this perspective, India could be expected to enjoy a natural leadership role in the region.

On the basis of India's regional dominance in size, military capabilities, and economic potential, much of the work on SAARC has been written from an India-specific perspective. For instance, O. P. Goel's comprehensive description of the SAARC summits is framed within the context of the importance of SAARC to the overall strategic objectives of India's foreign policy.[8] To be sure, India matters a great deal in South Asia. However, one can fall into the trap of merely viewing SAARC as an instrument of India's foreign policy, not as an institution for regional collaboration. In Chapter 1 I will show how from its foundation, SAARC has explicitly addressed the inherent regional asymmetry of power among SAARC members. Later in Chapter 3, I will address the perception that regional asymmetry is an impediment to collaboration, particularly in security and economic issues. In addition, I will argue that efforts at fostering regional cooperation are continually defeated under the pressure of internal rivalries in bilateral relations, particularly between India and Pakistan. In general, this inherent regional asymmetry has created a dichotomy between the way that India views itself in terms of global aspirations and how India's neighbors position themselves against what they perceive as India's overbearing, hegemonic stance in the region.

Other books about SAARC have attempted to break away from the constraints posed by viewing SAARC from an India-specific focal point. In my view, one of the most interesting scholarly contributions in that direction is Kishore Dash's *Regionalism in South Asia: Negotiating Cooperation, Institutional Structures.*[9] The book excels in providing clear cross-national comparisons and highlighting intraregional complementarities, but sadly only devotes one chapter to SAARC. This particular chapter focuses on the origins of the institution rather than on contemporary developments which are dealt with rather succinctly. Likewise, Ranjan Modi's *SAARC: Regional and Global Perspectives* is also a commendable example of this effort.[10] Despite its title, the book actually discusses little of the regional perspectives. Nevertheless, Modi devotes two (out of seven) chapters to international perspectives, namely those represented by the United States and Russia (and erstwhile Soviet Union). Although this book is commendable in its ambitions to internationalize the focus on SAARC, it focuses on one country (Russia) with only a peripheral relationship to SAARC. A more timely approach would instead focus on the countries that enjoy observer status (i.e., Australia, China, the European Union, Iran, Japan, Mauritius, Myanmar, South Korea, and the United States). One of these observer states, China, has declared its intention to become a fully fledged member of SAARC. Clearly, this would represent a major change in the internal dynamics of the association. However, no existing book on SAARC analyzes these intraregional developments.

On a broader level, other theoretical perspectives on regional integration delineate the obstacles to such integration on the basis of extending the membership rights beyond the core group of founding members. The enlargement of a regional body involves, as defined by Frank Schimmelfennig and Ulrich Sedelmeier, a process of gradual and formal horizontal institutionalization.[11] This process typically generates anxieties about the adaptation of existing substantive constraints on enhancing the membership structure. In recent years, for instance, a great deal of scholarly work and public debate has been generated on the rapid expansion of the membership in the European Community.[12] Likewise, on a much smaller scale, SAARC is vulnerable to these structural pressures. In Chapter 2 I will discuss the debates about SAARC enlargement and the incorporation of new countries as SAARC observers. Experience with the range of countries that have expressed an interest in attaining SAARC observer status or membership shows that

SAARC is ill-equipped to absorb the presence of new external actors. In my view, this represents a failure of institutional design and has important consequences for the future relevance of the association.

Scholarly analyses of the desirability of expanding membership could be confined to its instrumental components. Any expanding regional institution faces the standard collective action problems relating to the allocation of authority and sharing of administrative burdens to new actors. Nevertheless, in practice, debates about institutional enlargement typically revolve around more abstract normative considerations, such as democratic legitimacy or the potential loss of a collective regional identity. Will a cohesive European identity cease to exist if a predominantly Muslim country, like Turkey, joins the EU? Will South Asia cease to exist as a distinctive regional identity if, say, China or Iran join SAARC? It is difficult to answer these questions because few theoretical perspectives in political science treat identity formation seriously. Within the field of international relations theory, though, the constructivist literature provides a norms-based approach to the study of regional cooperation that restructures the theoretical debate in terms of the construction of identity. In this framework of analysis, the preferences of agents "are largely shaped by historically constructed identity norms."[13] In the constructivist approach, the norms that dominate specific institutions are bound by culture, namely "a set of collectively held prescriptions about the right way to think and act."[14] Chapter 2 will explore the ways in which SAARC enlargement can be understood.

Regional institutions can be analyzed by a set of complementary analytical approaches, but there is no comprehensive theoretical perspective that elucidates the importance of regional institutions. The neorealist literature eschews the importance of regional collaborative arrangements on issues that deal with internal security. In contrast, the neoliberal institutionalist literature may be helpful at highlighting the emergence of international norms that enhance the prospects for collaboration. In the absence of explicit incentives, the institutionalist literature suggests that regional institutions are unlikely to be an effective tool for multilateral cooperation.

Traditional systemic analyses of international relations tend to view the state as a central actor and referent in the discourse about challenges to security. However, recent innovations in international relations theory have broadened the security agenda and instead suggest that regional institutions and non-state actors play a vital role in the practice of security.[15] This framework of research, referred to as "securitization," has spawned a great deal of new analysis, particularly as it pertains to the new security challenges (e.g., terrorism, climate change, energy security, and health pandemics). In Chapter 3 I will also show that regional cooperation on security issues has been extremely limited. Instead, SAARC-led regional collaboration on security issues has been restricted to non-traditional ones. However, I will contend that such engagement has been more an expression of official intent rather than one of actual state policy.

While securitization remains a useful tool from which to begin analysis of new security challenges, fresh research has begun to offer critiques of this approach, mostly on the basis that the securitization framework has not adequately provided a comprehensive security analysis when applied to developing countries.[16] In such scenarios, any security analysis needs to consider the role of formal institutions and non-state actors as key security actors, particularly when they involve new security challenges affecting the state as well as non-state referent groups. Building upon the securitization literature, this book will attempt to fill the gap in the literature on SAARC by providing a clearer focus on the association's inner workings on issues relating to security and economic cooperation. To this effect, I will highlight the role of SAARC regional centers, namely specialized institutions that deal with key thematic concerns of SAARC's remit. To this effect, in Chapter 3 I will evaluate SAARC's efforts to understand the role of macrolevel institutions and non-state actors in addressing new forms of security challenges.

One of the principal achievements of SAARC has been the development of a South Asian Free Trade Agreement (SAFTA). Unfortunately, most available books about SAARC do not discuss this important development. An exception to this norm is D. K. Ghosh's *New Frontiers: Pathways for SAARC*.[17] Although Ghosh's work does a creditable job of evaluating the evolution of SAARC economies, it too fails to discuss SAFTA, chiefly because the book's publication predates the signing of the agreement. Likewise a volume edited by Anil Bhuimali and Chandan Mukhopadhyay, promisingly entitled *Economic Issues in SAARC Context*, offers a fairly detailed analysis of the principal macroeconomic issues facing different SAARC members, but once again, the focus is not on SAFTA, but rather on a quantitative analysis of macroeconomic trends.[18] Overall, these books fail to address issues relating to SAARC and their quantitative approaches to macroeconomic issues make them books of limited interest.[19] I will attempt to overcome this obstacle by highlighting themes that will engage a general audience. Chapter 3 will focus on the success of SAARC at starting a dialogue on economic cooperation. Subsequently, in Chapter 4 I illustrate the limited success of regional collaboration outside of security and economic issues.

Building on work by O. P. Goel, Dhirendra Dwivedi, Farhat Eshas, and Kishore Dash, one of the principal analytical parts of this book will evaluate the difficulties that formal regional institutions (such as the SAARC) have in enabling regional cooperation within the scope of security and economic cooperation. To this effect, I will focus on the efforts by SAARC to develop a common framework, namely through an integrated program of action (or IPA). As I will show in Chapter 4, the structural framework of SAARC has encouraged proposed cooperation on a diffuse array of issues, but it appears that there has been more clarity of purpose in taking active steps to foster cooperation on human capital and social infrastructure. I will point to the establishment of a South Asian University and a development bank as evidence of different patterns of tangible, albeit somewhat belated, collaboration outside of military and economic issues. Moreover, in Chapter 4 I will also address the efforts by SAARC to encourage regional cooperation through SAARC regional centers. These centers are specialized institutions that deal with the key thematic concerns of SAARC's general remit.

Based on the assumption that formal regional institutions may have failed to provide a solid institutional framework from which to address regional challenges, the final chapter of this book will offer some conclusions about the future challenges facing SAARC and the likely course of action that the association should take to overcome these obstacles. More importantly, though, I will also suggest some possible modalities of institutional changes that are likely to develop in the region. In many respects, SAARC cannot operate outside the self-imposed boundaries of its member states. However, in order to avoid being perceived as anachronistic, SAARC will need to consider becoming more adaptable to change. Despite its many problems, to use a comparative example, the transformation of the erstwhile Organization of African Unity (OAU) to the AU offers valuable lessons for how SAARC could develop.[20]

To conclude, authors write books operating under a vast number of informational constraints while responding to a wide range of conflicting incentives and personal pressures. This author is no different. It would be presumptuous to suggest that the stylized presentation of issues relating to SAARC, as developed in this book, will be a definitive statement about the association. My intention, though, is to make some suggestions for future avenues of research about SAARC that will be more theoretically informed and that will consider SAARC and other similar regional institutions from a truly comparative perspective. It is also hoped that other scholars will use SAARC as a case study, even if depicting the association as a failed regional institution. After all, we all learn from our failures as well as our successes.

# 1 SAARC membership and structure

- What is South Asia?
- Genesis of SAARC
- Founding of SAARC
- SAARC Charter
- SAARC organization
- SAARC summits
- Conclusion

In order to understand SAARC, one ought to consider that regional institutions often emerge on the basis of a shared regional awareness. As Andrew Hurrell reminds us, though, "'regional awareness', 'regional identity', and 'regional consciousness' are inherently imprecise and fuzzy notions."[1] Whether one understands regions on the basis of geographic contiguity, or cultural affinity, or economic interests, or on shared security concerns, the concept of a region denominated as "South Asia" certainly conforms to this imprecise definition of regions. In this chapter we will first explore the contours of South Asia, as defined geographically and culturally. We will then show how changing definitions about what constitutes South Asia helped shape the first efforts to create a regional institution in the region in the 1970s.

One of the more important developments in the initial stages of the formalization of a regional institution is the proposed design of that institution. In the case of SAARC, the key driver for the establishment of a South Asian regional institution was the leadership of a few political actors, principally Bangladesh's president, Ziaur Rahman. President Zia was instrumental in generating official support for a loose set of regional collaboration objectives which eventuated in the creation of SAARC. However, the narrative also shows that President Zia had mixed motives for embracing regional cooperation. Nevertheless, by taking a leadership role in drafting a proposal for regional collaboration,

President Zia—to use common terminology—acted as an "agenda setter." The SAARC Charter, the association's foundation document, bore the imprint of President Zia's vision for a South Asian regional institution.

In this chapter we will also explore the challenges that South Asian regional leaders faced when they agreed to hold the first summit of a loosely conceived South Asian regional organization. Moreover, we will show that the SAARC Charter contained a broad set of principles to guide regional collaboration. These principles made it difficult to implement any decisions reached at SAARC summits. To that effect, a SAARC Secretariat was established. In this chapter we will explore the basic organizational features of SAARC. We will pay particular attention to SAARC summits.

## What is South Asia?

South Asia is a heavily populated and highly heterogeneous region. Across the core group of countries typically designated as being part of South Asia, over 30 official languages are spoken. There are additional cleavages that differentiate South Asian countries, the religious and ethnic distinctions. Nevertheless, the region maintains a sense of cohesion on the basis of mutual colonial heritage. All the countries in South Asia are low-income countries. They also share other domestic attributes and characteristics.[2]

It may prove impossible to trace the exact etymology of the term "South Asia." Nevertheless, South Asia, as a distinctive geopolitical concept, began to be used by the United States Department of State in the late 1940s, following the independence of countries in the Indian subcontinent.[3] After 1947, the notion of South Asia began to be viewed as an entity that was distinct from the geographic unit under the colonial tutelage of Britain. As such, early academic usage of the term South Asia (or Southern Asia) highlighted a sense of disconnection between a new conception of the region and its previous configuration. Writing in 1950, one author argued that "South Asia of today is the child of revolution, of destructive energy, in contradistinction to the South Asia of yesterday, the child of the Suez Canal and the outcome of constructive effort."[4] Other authors conceptualized South Asia "as the belt of countries along the southern fringe of Asia from Pakistan to the Philippines, where colonialism has been a common characteristic, although Siam was included. Specifically, the countries that were considered are Pakistan, India, Ceylon, Burma, Siam (now, again, Thailand), Indochina, Malaya, Indonesia, and the Philippines."[5]

Subsequent academic usage of the concept of South Asia as a region began to draw an arbitrary line between South Asia and South East Asia, which had in common economic development problems but distinctive colonial heritages. Development economists began to write about South Asia as the sole focal point of their analysis or they began to discuss South Asia as a parallel developmental challenge to South East Asia.[6] In contemporary usage, the core group of South Asian nations includes Bangladesh, Bhutan, India, the Maldives, Nepal, Pakistan, and Sri Lanka. Some would also include Afghanistan, Burma, and Tibet. Afghanistan, as we shall show later, has deep historical, linguistic, cultural, and tribal connections to Pakistan and could reasonably be included as being part of South Asia, although typically it is depicted as being a Central Asian nation. The inclusion of Burma (or Myanmar) stems from the fact that Burma formed part of British India and only became a separate colonial entity in 1937. As a result of Myanmar's policy of isolation, the country's ongoing links to South Asia are faint. Although there are strong historical links between Tibet and the rest of the Indian subcontinent, the potential inclusion of Tibet as part of South Asia hinges on whether an individual accepts Tibet as an entity that is autonomous from China or whether one recognizes Chinese sovereignty over Tibet.

## Genesis of SAARC

There is considerable scholarly disagreement on the origins of the idea of establishing a framework for regional cooperation in South Asia. Some authors have suggested that the idea for the creation of an institution for regional cooperation was mulled over, prior to India and Pakistan's independence, at the March–April 1947 Inter-Asian Relations conference in New Delhi, India.[7] In contrast, other authors have stressed that subsequent diplomatic meetings, such as the Baguio conference in the Philippines in May 1950 and the Colombo Powers conference in April 1954 were among the more salient fora where the concept of forming a regional association was discussed.[8]

During the phase of postcolonial realignment, one of the most tangible proposals for multilateral regional cooperation in Asia was the enactment of the Colombo Plan for Cooperative and Social Development. Due to the inclusion of many South Asian countries in its inception, the Colombo Plan provided a model for the possibilities offered by multilateral engagement.[9] The Colombo Plan, however, was subsumed under the aegis of a larger institutional project, namely the Commonwealth.[10] As the nations of South Asia began to assert a more distinctive foreign policy away from their former colonial masters, Commonwealth-inspired institutions began to lose their appeal.

A third phase in the formation of a South Asia regional cooperation organization took place in the late 1970s. At the time, the emphasis was on the creation of a regional organization with a distinctive South Asian character and without direct links to overarching institutions like the Commonwealth. Between 1977 and 1980, Bangladesh's president Ziaur Rahman undertook a number of exploratory trips to India, Bangladesh, Nepal, Pakistan, and Sri Lanka for the purpose of discussing the parameters of a South Asian regional cooperation institution. In December 1977, during a three-country visit to Nepal, India, and Pakistan, President Zia presented a proposal for regional cooperation between Bangladesh and her neighbors, including an overland trade link between Bangladesh and Pakistan. The Bangladeshi press observed that President Zia found strong affinity with King Birendra of Nepal. For instance, an editorial in the *Bangladesh Times* commented that President Zia "viewed the evolution of an environment of peace as a necessary precondition to welfare in the region."[11]

During his December 1977 visit to India, President Zia substantively discussed the idea with India's prime minister Morarji Desai and foreign minister Atal Behari Vajpayee. The Indian government had been quite receptive to President Zia's call for greater regional integration, chiefly because Prime Minister Desai had been elected to head a loose coalition government in India. In order to cement the legitimacy of this coalition government in the region, the Indian government had launched a diplomatic offensive to improve India's relations with her neighbors. At the conclusion of the visit, a joint communiqué stressed the prospect for wider cooperation between the two countries.[12] In the midst of a proposal to declare the Indian Ocean a zone of peace, President Zia instead urged for the entire region of South Asia to be declared a zone of peace.[13]

During a period of martial law and consistent press censorship in Bangladesh, President Zia's proposal for greater regional integration was widely praised in the leading Bangladeshi press. Bangladeshi newspapers uncritically labeled the visit a great success in opening up the possibility of wider regional cooperation. For instance, the *Bangladesh Times* commented that President Zia's visit to India "had given new opportunities to work concertedly for peace and the reduction of armaments."[14] A few days later, another editorial in the same newspaper claimed that President Zia "has proved himself a successful advocate of regional peace and stability, good neighbourliness and unhindered national development following his visit to India, Pakistan and Nepal."[15] The

*Bangladesh Observer*, another of Bangladesh's leading dailies, also lavished praise on President Zia's accomplishments. An editorial in the *Bangladesh Observer* endorsed the view that "the visits, taken together, produced the propitious results they were intended to—namely an increased understanding by the sub-continental neighbors of the position of Bangladesh as a sovereign independent country pursuing consistently a policy of peace and good relations with all on the basis of mutual respect for independence, sovereign equality and non-interference in the internal affairs of the state."[16] Upon his return to Bangladesh, President Zia also endorsed the view that his state visits had been "positively successful" and, rather immodestly, asserted that they had been "significant to these countries and the region as a whole."[17]

The Indian press, however, was bemused by the true motives for President Zia's tour of the South Asian countries in December 1977. President Zia had seized power in April 1977, following a series of abortive military *coups d'état* in Bangladesh.[18] Therefore, there was some uncertainty as to the stability of his regime. Viewed in this context, an editorial in one of India's leading newspapers observed that the visits did not "seem to have been prompted by requirements of formal State relations. What President Zia seems to be seeking is more than formal acceptance of his position as Head of State; presumably, he wants to be recognized as a South Asia leader with as much credibility as anyone else."[19]

President Zia, however, was not alone in voicing the need for closer regional cooperation in South Asia. Likewise, King Birendra of Nepal also echoed this theme in a number of public appearances. For instance, in an inaugural speech to the Colombo Plan Consultative Committee, King Birendra called for closer regional cooperation under the auspices of a new regional institution. The subject was later broached during King Birendra's visit to Bangladesh in January 1978. According to Kishore Dash, in 1979 President Zia also discussed the idea of creating a South Asian regional cooperation organization during the Commonwealth summit in Lusaka, Zambia, and at the summit of the Non-Aligned Movement held in Havana, Cuba.[20]

It is clear that the perception that a regional cooperation organization for South Asia was a desirable option was being considered by the heads of state of several South Asian countries, notably Nepal and Bangladesh. Ultimately, though, the proposal for the creation of a South Asian regional forum was partially motivated by a number of internal considerations in Bangladesh. In an effort to reorient Bangladesh's foreign policy from an overt reliance on India, President Zia wished to broaden the scope of the country's allies and strategic partners. To that effect, he was drawn to the idea of Bangladesh joining ASEAN and he initiated steps to make that possible. Intellectually, the seminal proposal for the creation of SAARC on the basis of economic integration, as formulated by President Zia, was also influenced by an initiative from Shah A. M. S. Kibria, Bangladesh's foreign secretary from 1978 to 1981. Having served as a founding director of the Regional Cooperation for Development (RCD), a regional developmental agency established between Iran, Turkey, and Pakistan in July 1964, Kibria wanted to replicate this organization in South Asia.[21] According to Syed Muazzam Ali, Bangladesh's foreign secretary from 1999 to 2001, Kibria drafted the initial proposal outlining the justifications for the launching of a South Asian regional association.[22]

Bangladesh's bid to join ASEAN failed, whereupon a formal draft proposal to create a South Asian regional forum was drawn up by Bangladesh's president Ziaur Rahman. President Zia despatched special envoys to all the heads of state and government in South Asia with a letter dated 2 May 1980 in which he urged them to strongly consider the idea of creating a regional institution akin to ASEAN serving an economic cooperation zone for the region. South Asia's regional leaders provided detailed responses to President Zia's proposals, which were in turn evaluated by Bangladesh's Ministry of Foreign Affairs, and by November 1980 a document entitled *Paper on the Proposal for Regional Cooperation in South Asia* had been prepared and circulated.[23]

In response to this, the government of Sri Lanka agreed to convene a meeting of all the South Asian foreign secretaries, which duly took place on 13 February 1981. At the first SAARC summit in 1985, Bangladesh's foreign secretary Faruq Choudhury looked back at the evolution of the association and noted that "the first indication of the encouraging response of the six governments was available at an informal meeting of the Foreign Ministers of the seven countries during the non-aligned foreign ministers' meeting in New Delhi in 1981."[24] Two months later, the foreign secretaries of all seven countries in South Asia met again in Colombo, Sri Lanka, on 21–23 April 1981, just a month before President Zia's assassination.

Some countries were apprehensive about the Colombo meeting. For instance, India's foreign secretary, R. D. Sathe, was reported to have suggested that India "approached the proposal for a summit rather cautiously voicing the opinion that considerable sidework would have to be done before this by identifying areas of co-operation."[25] Contrary to expectations, the meeting turned out to be one of the most important to take place prior to the creation of SAARC. A joint communiqué issued at the end of the meeting set out concrete areas of cooperation that were mutually acceptable to all parties. More importantly, the tone set by the attendees indicated that disagreements could be aired respectfully. One commentator at the meeting observed that "despite the constraints of different kinds besetting the foreign secretaries it needs to be noted that the proceedings of the conference were marked by an extraordinary degree of mutual accommodation and appreciation of each other's point of view."[26] Nevertheless, another analyst observed that the foreign secretaries' meeting "revealed major differences between India and Pakistan on the one hand and the smaller countries on the other on the question of institutionalizing the regional cooperation scheme."[27]

The foreign secretaries' meetings led to a foreign ministers' meeting in New Delhi on 1–2 August 1983. According to one observer, the 1983 South Asian foreign ministers' meeting—the first of its kind in the region—"was remarkable for the atmosphere of cordiality and comradeship that pervaded it."[28] Although Imtiaz Bokhari argues that "no one expected dramatic breakthroughs," the delegates decided to adopt a Declaration on South Asian Regional Cooperation. The Declaration set out basic objectives and principles for South Asian regional cooperation and proposed some core institutional and financial arrangements.[29] The Declaration served to highlight the key areas of mutual cooperation that had emerged from the 1981 foreign secretaries' meeting in Colombo. The 1983 Declaration on South Asian Regional Cooperation spelt out seven objectives, three principles, and two general provisions.[30] As other authors have noted, the 1983 foreign ministers' meeting is significant because it was in this setting that the aims and objectives of that which evolved into SAARC were framed.[31] For instance, many sections of the text of the 1983 Declaration were eventually replicated verbatim in the SAARC Charter.

## Founding of SAARC

Following the 1983 foreign ministers' meeting in New Delhi, leaders from South Asia committed themselves to forming a regional institution. In consequence the first SAARC summit was held on December 7–8 1985.[32] Having been conceptualized by President Zia of Bangladesh, the first SAARC summit took place in Bangladesh. However, President Zia had been assassinated in May 1981, so the institutional leadership for this assembly was carried by Hussain Muhammad Ershad, the new president of Bangladesh.

The heads of state from the various South Asian countries represented at the first SAARC summit embodied a full spectrum of institutional governance frameworks and political systems. Two kings, Jigme Singye Wangchuk of Bhutan and Birendra Bir Bikram Shah Dev of Nepal, were among those heads of state represented at the summit. With the exception of India and (to a lesser extent) Sri Lanka, most countries in South Asia have not enjoyed a legacy of uninterrupted democratic rule.

During the first SAARC summit, India's prime minister, Rajiv Gandhi, represented an optimistic vision of parliamentary liberal democracy for the region. Meanwhile, Junius Richard Jayewardene, president of Sri Lanka at the time of the first SAARC summit, had been elected by popular vote in 1977, but then helped to restructure the Sri Lankan constitution to enable him to serve as executive president. Having granted himself unprecedented constitutional powers, President Jayewardene then barred the opposition presidential nominee, Sirimavo Bandaraike, from running for office. Moreover, he called a referendum to annul the result of the 1982 parliamentary election. The president of the Maldives, Maumoon Abdul Gayoom, had been nominated and selected by an intermediate electoral college called the Majlis. At the time of the first SAARC summit, President Gayoom had been re-elected with 96.62 percent of the vote in a referendum where he was the sole candidate for the presidency.[33] Finally, General Muhammad Zia-ul-Haq, the president of Pakistan, had ousted Pakistan's first democratically elected prime minister in a *coup d'état* and acquired the office of president, a post he held until his death in 1988. In general, the significant variation in the institutionalization of democracy across South Asia, as exemplified by the delegates to the first SAARC summit, poses a challenge to SAARC given that political consensus among the participant member states is likely to be required.

## SAARC Charter

The first SAARC summit included the heads of state from seven South Asian countries (i.e., Bangladesh, Bhutan, India, the Maldives, Nepal, Pakistan, and Sri Lanka). The meeting was structured to enhance an ambiance of mutual cooperation on the basis of a deviation from the legacy of a shared colonial heritage. During the prelude to the summit, Bangladesh's foreign minister Humayun Choudhury declared that the first SAARC summit "will create an atmosphere which will reverse the process injected into South Asia by colonial powers and intensified by the countries themselves after those powers had left."[34] In an unusual departure from the tedium of diplomatic summitry, speeches were sprinkled with poetry. For instance, Prime Minister Rajiv Gandhi read verses (in Bengali) from Kazi Nazrul Islam's poem, "Chalo re chalo re chalo"

("Let's go, let's go, let's go"). According to press reports, Rajiv Gandhi's reading of the poem drew "heavy applause from those assembled."[35] Not to be outdone, President Ershad released a poem entitled "Seven Perfumed Prospects."[36] The poem read in part:

The dream celebrating the noble goal
Reveals the shared faith
Reared in the sanctuary of the soul
Of South Asia, the Seven perfumed prospects
Now united in the alliance of honour.
...
The history, tradition and glory of civilisation
Will restore life's lost rhythmic theme
The familiar footsteps will revive their motion
And the passion to reshape the living scheme
On the occasion of SARC summit.

Against the backdrop of poetry, press reports from India took a predictably more jaundiced view of the first SAARC summit. For instance, the *Hindustan Times*, one of India's most respected dailies, opined that controversial bilateral issues between India and Pakistan—particularly over the issue of Kashmir—would overshadow any potential collaborative endeavors that might emerge via the institutional mechanism provided by SAARC. An editorial in the *Hindustan Times* argued that "Pakistani leaders have hardly ever missed an opportunity to raise the question of Kashmir whenever they can."[37] Another commentator reacted with sarcasm to the implicit criticisms made by the president of Pakistan, Zia-ul-Haq. In a critical response to the late President Zia's commitment to SAARC, N. C. Menon posited that "it would be interesting to watch [to see if] Pakistan, a signatory to the Charter, can jell the anti-terrorist practice of training Sikh terrorists in Pakistani camps before unleashing them into Punjab."[38]

The delegates to the first SAARC summit formally adopted the SAARC Charter, the association's principal governing document. The SAARC Charter is divided into 10 articles and includes a preamble. In the preamble, the signatories to the Charter pledged to promote "peace, stability, amity and progress in the region through strict adherence to the principles of the UNITED NATIONS CHARTER and NON-ALIGNMENT" [emphasis in the original]. The preamble to the SAARC Charter also embraced general principles of "sovereign equality, territorial integrity, national independence, non-use of force and non-interference in the internal affairs of other States and peaceful settlement of all disputes."[39]

As a governing document, the bulk of the SAARC Charter provides some guidance of the objectives, aims, and principles of the association. For instance, Article 1 of the Charter outlines a set of broad objectives which include:

- to promote the welfare of the peoples of SOUTH ASIA and to improve their quality of life [emphasis in the original];
- to accelerate economic growth, social progress and cultural development in the region and to provide all individuals the opportunity to live in dignity and to realise their full potentials;
- to promote and strengthen collective self-reliance among the countries of SOUTH ASIA [emphasis in the original];
- to contribute to mutual trust, understanding and appreciation of one another's problems;
- to promote active collaboration and mutual assistance in the economic, social, cultural, technical and scientific fields;
- to strengthen cooperation with other developing countries;
- to strengthen cooperation among themselves in international forums on matters of common interests; and
- to cooperate with international and regional organisations with similar aims and purposes.[40]

These objectives were identical to the objectives adopted at the first foreign ministers' meeting held on 1–2 August 1983. Likewise, Article 2 of the SAARC Charter sets out the broad principles that govern the association, and which are identical to the principles that were outlined in the 1983 meeting. These include:

- Cooperation within the framework of the Association shall be based on respect for the principles of sovereign equality, territorial integrity, political independence, non-interference in the internal affairs of other States and mutual benefit;
- Such cooperation shall not be a substitute for bilateral and multilateral cooperation but shall complement them; and
- Such cooperation shall not be inconsistent with bilateral and multilateral obligations.[41]

## SAARC organization

Beyond a broad range of objectives, aims, and principles (see above), the SAARC Charter does not provide a great deal of guidance on its

**Box 1.1 The SAARC Charter (key points)**

***Purposes***

- Promotion of peace, stability and amity within the region
- Advance in welfare and improvement of quality of life
- National and collective self-reliance
- Acceleration of economic growth, social progress and cultural development
- Mutual assistance in economic, social, cultural, technical and scientific fields
- Cooperation with other developing countries
- Cooperation between member states in international forums on matters of common interest
- Cooperation with international and regional organizations with similar aims

***Principles***

- Respect for the principles of sovereign equality, territorial integrity, political independence
- Renunciation of the use or threat of force
- Non-interference in the internal affairs of other member states
- Peaceful settlement of all disputes
- Complement to bilateral and multilateral cooperation in the region

***Decision-making***

- Decisions at all levels based on unanimity
- Bilateral and contentious issues are excluded from deliberations
- Meetings of the Heads of State or Government (summits) as highest level of decision-making

Source: Extracted from the Charter of the South Asian Association for Regional Cooperation (available at: www.saarc-sec.org/SAARC-Charter/5).

structure and organization. A curious feature of SAARC is its explicit design to encourage consensus and to minimize the discussion of contentious issues. For instance, Article 10 of the SAARC Charter delineates only two general provisions. The first provision is that "decisions at all levels shall be taken on the basis of unanimity."[42] In a region where sharp disagreements on a wide number of issues are prevalent, the SAARC Charter provides that "bilateral and contentious issues shall be excluded from the deliberations."[43]

Underscoring the egalitarian approach to membership rights and collective, consensus-driven, decision-making mechanisms, the highest authority of SAARC rests with the heads of state of all the member states of this regional body. Article 3 of the SAARC Charter specifies that the heads of state or government of all the SAARC member states must meet at least once a year, or more often as may be considered necessary by the member states.[44] In practice, however, formal annual meetings of all the member states of SAARC are irregular. Instead, SAARC summits, held every two years, ultimately serve as the principal forum uniting all the heads of state from South Asia.

The apex leadership body composed of all the heads of state of South Asia is assisted by a Council of Ministers. Article 4 of the SAARC Charter provides that this Council is composed of the foreign ministers of all the member states. The SAARC Charter specifies that this body is responsible for formulating policies, reviewing progress, deciding on new areas of cooperation, establishing additional mechanisms as deemed necessary, and deciding on other matters of general interest to the association.[45]

At a secondary level, the Council of Ministers is to be assisted in the execution of its duties by a Standing Committee. According to Article 5 of the SAARC Charter, membership to the Standing Committee is to be provided to all the foreign secretaries of the SAARC member states. Article 5 provides that the Standing Committee is to have the following functions:

- overall monitoring and coordination of program of cooperation;
- approval of projects and programs, and the modalities of their financing;
- determination of inter-sectoral priorities;
- mobilization of regional and external resources; and
- identification of new areas of cooperation based on appropriate studies.[46]

The SAARC Charter envisioned that the Standing Committee would be a particularly proactive body within SAARC. Article 5 of the Charter specifies that the Standing Committee "shall meet as often as deemed necessary."[47] Moreover, Article 5 specifies that the remit of the Standing Committee shall be to "submit periodic reports to the Council of Ministers and make reference to it as and when necessary for decisions on policy matters."[48] In addition, as will be discussed later in this chapter, the Standing Committee plays an important role in the structure of SAARC summits.

In light of the association's driving mechanism to mandate unanimity in the decision-making process, it would be anticipated that from a public policy perspective coordination and implementation issues would be of paramount importance. The SAARC Charter provides for the establishment of a coordination and implementation unit called the Technical Committees. Article 6 provides that the Technical Committees "shall be responsible for the implementation, coordination and monitoring of the programmes in their respective areas of cooperation."[49] The terms of reference of the Technical Committees are also outlined in Article 6 of the SAARC Charter. These include:

- determination of the potential and the scope of regional cooperation in agreed areas;
- formulation of programs and preparation of projects;
- determination of financial implications of sectoral programs;
- formulation of recommendations regarding apportionment of costs;
- implementation and coordination of sectoral programs; and
- monitoring of progress in implementation.[50]

Keeping in line with the association's egalitarianism, the Charter provides that the Chairmanship of the Technical Committees "shall normally rotate among Member States in alphabetical order every two years."

The SAARC Charter mandates the Technical Committees to submit periodic reports to the Standing Committee.[51] In order to fulfil its mandate, the SAARC Charter enables the Technical Committees to use a wide range of mechanisms and modalities, including:

- meetings of heads of national technical agencies;
- meetings of experts in specific fields; and
- contact among recognized centers of excellence in the region.

Moreover, the SAARC Charter enables the Technical Committees to set up ad hoc Action Committees "comprising Member States concerned with implementation of projects involving more than two but not all Member States."[52] The Technical Committees formulate programs and prepare projects in their respective fields of expertise. As will be discussed in more detail in Chapter 4, the projects developed by the Technical Committees emerge from defined areas of collaboration in SAARC's Integrated Programme of Action (see Figure 1.1).

On a day-to-day basis, much of the actual work involving SAARC is directed from its secretariat. Unfortunately, the SAARC Charter did not provide a detailed mandate for the secretariat as originally proposed.

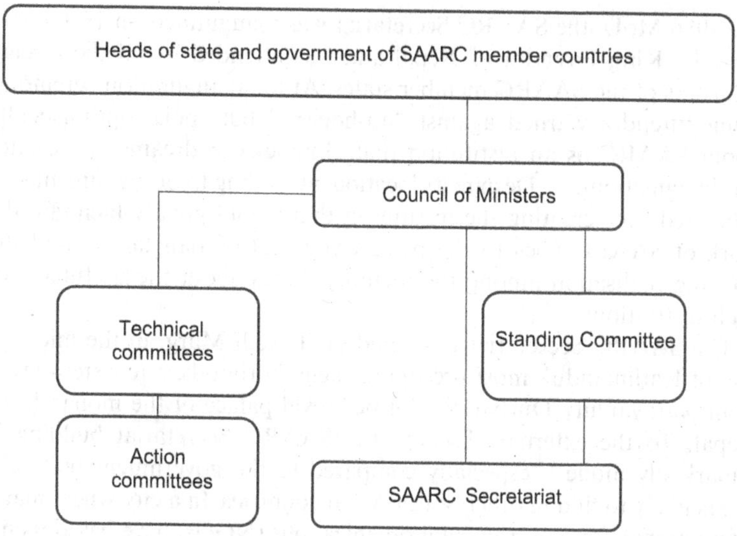


*Figure 1.1* Flowchart of general SAARC structure
Source: SAARC Secretariat

Article 8 of the SAARC Charter merely states, rather parsimoniously, that "there shall be a Secretariat of the Association."[53] The absence of a formal secretariat indicated a lack of institutionalization of the association prior to the first SAARC summit. Before the start of that summit, while addressing the fourth meeting of South Asia's foreign ministers, Bangladesh's foreign minister, Humayun Rasheed Choudhury, had stressed the vital need to establish a permanent secretariat. Nevertheless, the summit's spokesman, Abul Ahsan, noted that the question of setting up a SAARC secretariat would be taken up after the formal launching of the forum.[54]

The Standing Committee of Foreign Secretaries informally mulled over the idea of establishing a permanent secretariat in Nepal or Bangladesh. However, during the first SAARC summit, it was acknowledged by Abul Ahsan that only Nepal had offered to host a SAARC secretariat, but stressed that the eventual secretariat would be planned according to recommendations by the SAARC Council of Ministers.[55] Subsequently, a Memorandum of Understanding (MoU) on the Establishment of the Secretariat was signed on 17 November 1986 between the foreign secretaries of all the SAARC member states.[56] The MoU provided for the basic structural elements of the SAARC Secretariat. Based on the provisions of the 1986 MoU, a permanent SAARC Secretariat was to be established in Kathmandu, Nepal. A few months after the signing of the 1986 MoU, the SAARC Secretariat was inaugurated on 16 January 1987 by King Birendra of Nepal and was attended by all the foreign ministers of the SAARC member states. At the inauguration ceremony, King Birendra warned against "ad-hocism" but spoke optimistically about SAARC as an institution that "kindles our dreams and excites our imaginations."[57] Despite its location, according to one commentator, "the credit for creating the institution that would greatly facilitate the work of SAARC goes to the persevering zeal of Bangladesh and the growing realisation among the member States about the usefulness of such institutions."[58]

The SAARC Secretariat is located on Trivedi Marg, in the midst of one of Kathmandu's most prestigious neighborhoods, a few steps away from Narayanhity Durbar, the former royal palace of the monarchs of Nepal. To the external observer, the SAARC Secretariat building is remarkably modest, especially compared to the government buildings one is likely to find in other South Asian countries. In a city where many international non-governmental organizations (NGOs) have based themselves in impressively sized buildings, the discreet, two-story bungalow-style SAARC Secretariat building is reminiscent of a political party headquarters or the site of a second-tier ministry. The no-frills interior of the building is spotlessly clean, but one does not get the sense that there is a great deal of official business taking place throughout the day. Nevertheless, the staff based at the secretariat appear to be capable, attentive and responsive, lacking the bureaucratic somnolescence one can typically anticipate finding in government buildings across South Asia.

The 1986 MoU on the Establishment of the Secretariat provided for the appointment of a secretary general. According to Article 5 of the 1986 MoU, the secretary general is to be appointed by the SAARC Council of Ministers based on the nomination "by a Member State on the basis of the principle of rotation in alphabetical order." Initially, the tenure for this post was limited to two years. Commenting critically on this restriction, Abul Ahsan, SAARC's first secretary general, argued that the "two year non-renewable tenure of the SAARC Secretary General hardly allows him to grow in the post to enable him to make an effective contribution to the organization."[59] Subsequently, Article 5 of the SAARC declaration issued at the ninth SAARC summit in Malé, Maldives, provided that the tenure of the secretary general shall be for a non-renewable term of three years.[60]

Article 8 of the 1986 MoU on the Establishment of the Secretariat outlines the functions and powers of the SAARC secretary general and provides a more precise structural framework for the composition and aims of the SAARC Secretariat. Broadly, the secretary general's powers are circumscribed by the Standing Committee and by the Council of Ministers. For instance, the secretary general is expected to report regularly to the Standing Committee and to submit the secretariat's annual budget to the Standing Committee for approval by the Council of Ministers. In a critical overview of the institutional framework of the SAARC Secretariat, O. P. Shah noted that as the association's activities expanded "the work of the Secretary General has increased manifold." In his view, "the workload is approaching a level where he may find it very difficult, if not impossible, to discharge his responsibilities effectively."[61]

One of the striking structural features of the association is its financing mechanism. Article 9 of the SAARC Charter provides for the financial arrangements of the association. In this financial set-up, "the contribution of each Member State towards financing of the activities of the Association shall be voluntary."[62] The SAARC Charter entrusts each Technical Committee to "make recommendations for the apportionment of costs of implementing the programmes proposed by it."[63] Anticipating that a voluntary financing mechanism may not be an optimal structure to tackle unanticipated exogenous shocks, the SAARC Charter specifies that "in case sufficient financial resources cannot be mobilised within the region for funding activities of the Association, external financing from appropriate sources may be mobilised with the approval of or by the Standing Committee."[64]

In the operational functioning of the association, the SAARC secretary general plays an important role. Formally, the secretary general's powers include responsibility for conducting the work of the secretariat including the coordination and monitoring of SAARC activities and acting as a channel of communication and linkage between SAARC and other international organizations. However, as Article 8 specifies, the secretary general "shall be guided by the decision of the Council of Ministers that initiatives for collaboration with external agencies should stem from SAARC itself based on its own determination of priorities and keeping in mind the relevant provisions of the SAARC Charter."[65]

Although SAARC has been subject to criticism about its effectiveness, there is no doubt that this regional body is viewed among diplomats from South Asia as a prestigious institution. Accordingly, SAARC secretaries general nominated by their countries have all been distinguished diplomats (see Table 1.1). Given that controversial subject matters may not be broached at SAARC summits, it is no surprise that SAARC secretaries general have maintained a low public profile while in office.

*Table 1.1* SAARC secretaries general

| *Name* | *Country* | *Tenure of Service* |
|---|---|---|
| Abul Ahsan | Bangladesh | 16 January 1987 to 15 October 1989 |
| Kant Kishore Bhargava | India | 17 October 1989 to 31 December 1991 |
| Ibrahim Hussain Zaki | Maldives | 1 January 1992 to 31 December 1993 |
| Yadav Kant Silwal | Nepal | 1 January 1994 to 31 December 1995 |
| Naeem Hasan | Pakistan | 1 January 1996 to 31 December 1998 |
| Nihal Rodrigo | Sri Lanka | 1 January 1999 to 10 January 2002 |
| Q. A. M. A. Rahim | Bangladesh | 11 January 2002 to 28 February 2005 |
| Lyonpo Chenkyab Dorji | Bhutan | 1 March 2005 to 29 February 2008 |
| Sheel Kant Sharma | India | 1 March 2008 to the 28 February 2011 |
| Uz. Fathimath Dhiyana | Maldives | 1 March 2011 to the present |

A notable exception to this pattern has been the case of the third SAARC secretary general, Ibrahim Hussain Zaki. Having returned to the Maldives, Zaki became an increasingly prominent member of the political opposition to President Gayoom. He defected from President Gayoom's cabinet and overnight became one of the most vociferous politicians of the Maldivian Democratic Party (MDP). In 2004 he was imprisoned for his involvement in a pro-democracy rally staged in protest over alleged human rights abuses in the Maldives.

The SAARC secretary general is assisted by a Professional and a General Services Staff. According to Article 6 of the MoU on the Establishment of the Secretariat, the members of the Professional Staff "shall be appointed by the Secretary General upon nomination by Member States."[66] In turn, the secretary general exercises some discretion in hiring the requisite members of the General Services Staff for the normal administrative functioning of the secretariat. The MoU on the Establishment of the Secretariat specifies that the General Services Staff should be nationals of SAARC member states and recruited through advertised open competition.[67] In contrast to other administrative appointments to the SAARC Secretariat, no restrictions are placed on the length of time in which the General Services Staff may serve. In essence, the General Services Staff constitutes the association's civil service.

Member states maintain an important link to the operational activities of the SAARC Secretariat, primarily through their involvement in the SAARC Secretariat's Working Divisions. The SAARC Secretariat is divided into eight working divisions. The Working Divisions include: media and integration of Afghanistan; agriculture and rural development; environment and biotechnology; economic, trade and finance; social affairs; information and poverty alleviation; energy, tourism, and science; and, human resource development, security aspects, and culture (see Figure 1.2).

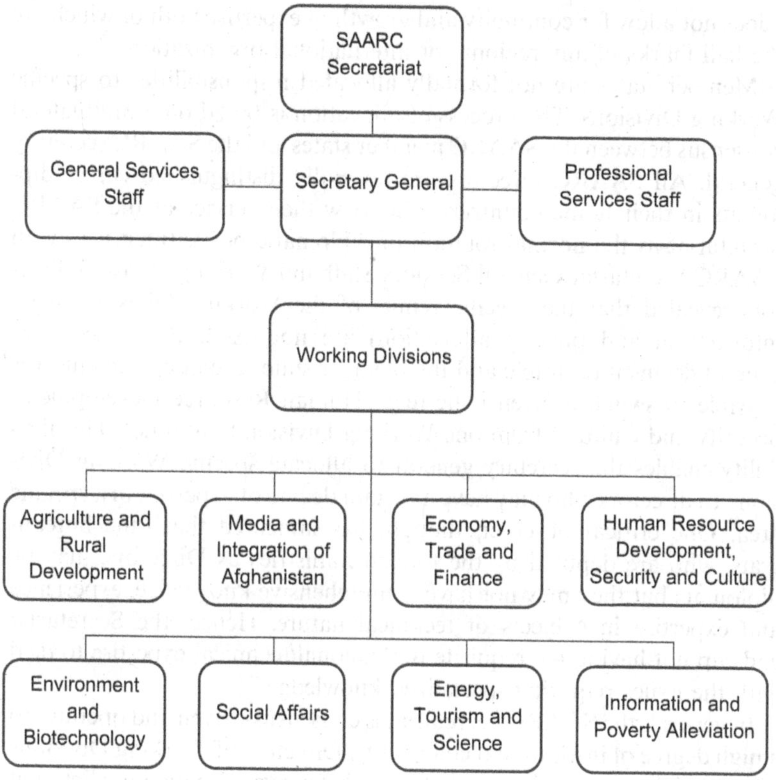


*Figure 1.2* Flowchart of SAARC Secretariat
Source: SAARC Secretariat

Each member state has the power to nominate one officer to the level of director who, on appointment, is expected to take charge of a Working Division to be assigned by the secretary general. Article 6 of the MoU on the Establishment of the Secretariat provides that the appointment of a director of a Working Division shall be limited to three years. However, the secretary general may, in consultation with the member state concerned, extend the tenure for a period not exceeding another full term.[68] In practice, though, this particular privilege has rarely been exercised. Reflecting on his experience as a SAARC secretary general, Abul Ahsan argued that "as SAARC grows consideration may be given to recruit Directors on a regional basis taking into account their qualification and experience. They should be either permanent employees of the Secretariat or serve there for a longer period."[69] In Ahsan's view, the practice of limiting the tenure of SAARC directors "does not allow for continuity and growth of expertise both of which are the hall marks of any regional or international organization."[70]

Member states are not formally allocated responsibilities to specific Working Divisions. The process of allocation is based on a multilateral consensus between the SAARC member states and the SAARC secretary general. All SAARC directors are normally distinguished career diplomats in their home countries, who view their service at the SAARC Secretariat as the normal rotation of diplomatic posts. Interviews with SAARC Secretariat General Services Staff and Working Division directors revealed that the specific remits of the Working Divisions (e.g., information and poverty alleviation) are not fixed. If the secretary general deems it desirable and the member states are in agreement, it is possible to switch a given issue (e.g., Human Resource Development, Security and Culture) from one Working Division to another. This flexibility enables the secretary general to allocate specific Working Divisions to directors who may have a certain degree of expertise in a specific area. One critical observer, though, has lamented that "the bureaucrats, who are deputed by the foreign ministries as Directors, may be diplomats but they may not have comprehensive knowledge, experience and expertise in subjects of technical nature. Hence, the Secretariat ends up not having the requisite professional/technical expertise to deal with the issues requiring specialized knowledge."[71]

In general, the SAARC Secretariat is consensus-driven and operates to a high degree of institutional collegiality. Directors of Working Divisions often collaborate on issues that may have overlapping jurisdictional domains, so this tends to reinforce the collegial environment among Working Division directors. Given that directors are official representatives of their member state countries, it is inevitable that a particular government's official policy may clash with initiatives sponsored by the SAARC Secretariat. In essence, directors of Working Divisions have to walk a fine line between representing the interests of their home government with the approaches adopted by all SAARC member states. Thus, whenever a member state disagrees with any aspect of a SAARC initiative, this serves as an implicit veto on any action taking place.

At an operational level, the primary function of the Working Division directors is to organize meetings (between summits) around specific issues where multilateral collaboration may be possible. Thus, the SAARC Secretariat, via its Working Divisions, enables multilateral collaboration to emerge in informal settings, prior to their potential examination at a SAARC summit. The meetings organized by Working Division directors also serve another purpose, which is to filter out potential issues that could prove contentious or problematic at a later stage. During such meetings it may become evident that some issues (albeit not necessarily controversial) are, in reality, bilateral issues. Since the association eschews the discussion of issues of exclusively bilateral relevance at SAARC summits, SAARC directors cannot mandate individual member states to adopt any given policy without the unanimous consent of all member states. Thus, if a member state wishes to prevent a particular issue from being raised at a SAARC summit, then all that is necessary is to signal to the SAARC Secretariat that it falls outside the association's jurisdiction. In this way, member states can exercise an informal veto on SAARC approved policy initiatives.

At the conclusion of a meeting sponsored by a SAARC Working Division, a report is prepared for presentation to the SAARC Standing Committee. The Standing Committee has the mandate to approve the discussion of an issue at a SAARC summit. At times, however, there are specific issues that the SAARC Standing Committee may deem to be potentially contentious. Rather than rejecting a proposal adopted at a Working Division, the Standing Committee simply requests the Division to conduct an additional review. This referral serves as an important signal that a particular issue may be too controversial for discussion at a SAARC summit.

## SAARC summits

Undoubtedly, the showcase event of SAARC is the association's summit, typically held every two years. Between the inaugural SAARC 1985 summit and the 2010 summit, a total of 16 summits has been held (see Table 1.2).

Both the SAARC Secretariat and the Working Divisions play a particularly important role in the design of each summit. The secretariat selects potential issues of interest to be discussed at the summit, and advises the country convening the summit on its precise framework. Eventually, the secretariat provides guidance to a programming committee that is set up in advance of the actual summit.

The programming committee examines the calendar of activities in excruciating detail primarily to allow the summit to operate flawlessly and to circumvent any issues that might prove contentious. At that point, the SAARC secretary general assists in the selection of issues approved at the Standing Committee or themes (often discussed during Working Division meetings) to be formally discussed at the summit.[72]

The Standing Committee then draws up a draft of the agenda to be discussed at the summit and presents it at the foreign secretaries' meeting that precedes all SAARC summits. Subsequently, a foreign ministers' meeting takes place when the proposed agenda is evaluated. Ministers have the option to approve the agenda in its entirety or to refer some issues

*Table 1.2* List of SAARC summits

| | *City* | *Country* | *Date* |
|---|---|---|---|
| 1st | Dhaka | Bangladesh | 7–7 December 1985 |
| 2nd | Bangalore | India | 16–17 November 1986 |
| 3rd | Kathmandu | Nepal | 2–4 November 1987 |
| 4th | Islamabad | Pakistan | 29–31 December 1988 |
| 5th | Malé | Maldives | 21–23 November 1990 |
| 6th | Colombo | Sri Lanka | 21 December 1991 |
| 7th | Dhaka | Bangladesh | 10–11 April 1993 |
| 8th | New Delhi | India | 2–4 May 1995 |
| 9th | Malé | Maldives | 12–14 May 1997 |
| 10th | Colombo | Sri Lanka | 29–31 July 1998 |
| 11th | Kathmandu | Nepal | 4–6 January 2002 |
| 12th | Islamabad | Pakistan | 4–6 January 2004 |
| 13th | Dhaka | Bangladesh | 12–13 November 2005 |
| 14th | New Delhi | India | 3–4 April 2007 |
| 15th | Colombo | Sri Lanka | 1–3 August 2008 |
| 16th | Thimpu | Bhutan | 28–29 April 2010 |

back to the Standing Committee for further review. Finally, before the arrival of all the SAARC heads of state, the foreign ministers meet to approve the agenda following its endorsement at the foreign secretaries' meeting. The timeline between the meeting of the programming committee and the meeting of the heads of state at a SAARC summit is typically three days.

As a result of the SAARC Secretariat's procedures and the association's self-adopted objective not to discuss contentious issues, SAARC summits tend to be well organized, but can appear to be bland affairs. A SAARC summit typically lasts for two or three days and revolves around a broad theme. At the conclusion of each summit, the SAARC member states issue a declaration which addresses the overarching theme of the summit, but also announces broad initiatives on other issues. In parallel to this, the SAARC member states also release a joint press release which summarizes the main agreements reached. Occasionally, at the conclusion of SAARC summits, SAARC member states reach a formal agreement on specific policy issues, and conventions on other policy issues are also signed.[73] Between 1985 and 2000 only four agreements or conventions were signed by SAARC member states. From 2000 onwards, however, there has been—in relative terms—an explosion of such activity. Between 2000 and 2010 nine agreements or conventions were signed by SAARC member states, including an additional protocol to one of the earliest regional conventions. In general, SAARC activity revolves around its summits, but there is clearly scope for improvement. For instance, a report prepared by the SAARC group of eminent persons suggested that SAARC "summits should be made more business-like and functional, which could be achieved by convening executive sessions and cutting down on ceremonial aspects."[74]

## Conclusion

In this chapter we have evaluated the events leading to the creation of SAARC. We showed that the formalization of regional institutional arrangements in South Asia followed three stages, from the immediate period of independence from Britain, through an era of postcolonial realignment, concluding with the institutionalization of a South Asian specific regional character. One of the most important considerations in the analysis of an emerging regional architecture in South Asia was the proposed institutional design. In the case of SAARC, the key driver for the establishment of a South Asian regional institution was the leadership by a few political actors, principally Bangladesh's president Ziaur Rahman. President Zia was instrumental in generating official support for a loose set of regional collaboration objectives which eventuated in the creation of SAARC.

The chapter traced some of the pivotal developments in the creation of SAARC, notably in the drafting of the 1983 Declaration on South Asian Regional Cooperation and subsequently during its first summit in 1985. The first SAARC summit led to a number of important agreements, principally the SAARC Charter, the association's foundational document. In this chapter we outlined some of the key features of this document. The SAARC Charter contains a broad set of principles to guide regional collaboration. However, on its own it provided little practical guidance that could be translated into concrete policy outcomes. To remedy that inconsistency, the association eventually established a secretariat. In this chapter we delineated some of the principal organizational features of this body and its associated institutions. The SAARC Secretariat is important insofar as it channels the work of the association, culminating in intermittent SAARC summits.

It is important to understand the formal aspects of SAARC. Elsewhere in the book, however, we will show that informal elements shape the growth of this regional body. For instance, key elements in the SAARC Charter itself constrain specific actions from taking place, whether they be in the realm of security and economic cooperation or in collaboration on social capital and infrastructure. As one analyzes the outcomes from SAARC summit declarations, the institutional timidity comes to the fore. In the absence of a coherent institutional design, we will later show that many of the association's perceived weaknesses stem from this initial stage of regional development.

# 2 The enlargement of SAARC

- Regionalism and multilateralism
- Country specificity: Afghanistan joins SAARC
- SAARC observers
- SAARC's relations with intergovernmental organizations
- Conclusion

SAARC, like other regional and multilateral institutions, has struggled to enlarge its membership. This phenomenon should not be surprising to students of institutions. On the one hand, rationalist and public choice theoretical approaches to the study of institutions would suggest that distributional conflicts and political tensions are likely to arise during an enlargement process on the basis of the expected redistribution of enlargement gains and relative losses after expansion. At the same time, although governments may be expected to pursue self-interested preferences and goals, it is also possible to understand the association's enlargement process from a more informal desire to expand common regional values and norms. So far, SAARC has expanded its membership once, but as we will see, there are continuing pressures from other countries to join this regional body.

In this chapter I will attempt to strike a middle ground between the formal and informal components of the enlargement of SAARC, largely by drawing attention to those international actors that have been eager to engage with SAARC. Using this approach, I will first focus on the countries that enjoy observer status to the association. I will discuss the challenges faced by countries that have attempted to join SAARC, thus far unsuccessfully. I will also explore SAARC's interactions with other multilateral institutions.

## Regionalism and multilateralism

Given that its membership structure appears to be defined by geographical contiguity, SAARC is widely recognized as a regional institution.

However, the distinction between regional institutions and multilateralism is a nuanced one in international relations theory. For instance, a multilateral organization, using John Ruggie's definition, is "defined by such generalized decision-making rules as voting or consensus procedures."[1] This would suggest that SAARC also has the capacity of being conceived as a multilateral organization, with a focus that could extend beyond the constraints of a region. Similarly, the presence of voting or consensus procedures is not a sufficiently rigorous manner in which to distinguish between regional or multilateral institutions. Most multilateral institutions have voting procedures, but some do not. For instance, at its inception the United Nations Conference on Trade and Development (UNCTAD) had elaborate voting procedures, but over time these have been discarded. Likewise, the UN Conference on the Law of the Sea was viewed as a radical step in decision-making by consent in that it did not involve recourse to voting.[2] In this sense, it would be more accurate to view SAARC as a multilateral organization, with a definition that implies more than two state members.

When we examine SAARC on the basis of its functions, we are tempted to compare it to every emerging institution that faces critical challenges in its development. We know that other regional institutions, such as the Shanghai Cooperation Organization (SCO), have altered their initial institutional aims and objectives as a consequence of their enlargement.[3] Likewise, international institutions, like the EU or the North Atlantic Treaty Organization (NATO), have been redefined and transformed through enlargement.[4] In this chapter, I will explore the challenges that SAARC has faced with respect to its own enlargement within a South Asian regional framework, but as I shall show there is increasing demand to expand the focus of the association beyond the existing regional parameters.

During the initial stages of institutionalization, there is an inherent tension between the existing institutional arrangements (e.g., the component national currencies before a monetary union is formed, or the constituent colonial administrative units prior to the end of the colonial period) and the transforming institutional modalities (e.g., the initial adoption of the euro in 2002, or the post-independence landscape in South Asia after 1947). However, associations—like SAARC—which do not entail the destruction or replacement of existing institutions, face the added challenge of legitimizing the emerging institution in a setting where competing institutions are in existence. It is along this transitional phase that emerging institutions are viewed through the prism of existing institutions.

As one evaluates SAARC, it is important to note that much of the analysis of the association is motivated by an effort to understand how it advances certain country specific foreign policy objectives. In fact, as has been pointed out in the introduction to this book, one of the inherent weaknesses in the literature on SAARC has been its narrow country focus, mostly framed within the context of the importance of the association within the overall strategic objectives of India's foreign policy.[5] Curiously, there are conspicuously few books on SAARC from the perspective of other South Asian countries, including those whose foreign policy goals (e.g., Bangladesh) have been closely linked to the association.[6] Moreover, it is safe to suggest that South Asians do not view SAARC or even themselves as being part of a meaningful community, compared to, say, how Europeans may view themselves as forming part of the European Union. It is also striking to note that the enlargement of SAARC has been a largely neglected issue in the analysis of regional integration in South Asia.

More importantly, though, the discussion about the enlargement of SAARC also raises fundamental theoretical questions about state identity formation and the building of regional identity. Mainstream international relations theory typically eschews the importance of identity, or at least relegates it to a single identity. In the neorealist paradigm, for instance, state identity is equated with the state's interest as a self-interested actor. In contrast, Ted Hopf, Alexander Wendt, and other constructivists have offered an alternative understanding for the relationship between state identity and interest. From the constructivist perspective, identity is viewed as a mechanism to explain state practice, interests, and interactions internationally. According to Hopf, constructivism assumes that "the selves, or identities, of states are a variable; they likely depend on historical, cultural, political, and social context."[7] In this framework, identity is understood to be a "particular set of interests or preferences with respect to choices of action in particular domains, and with respect to particular actors."[8] Hopf then adds that identities "offer each state an understanding of other states, its nature, motives, interests, probable actions, attitudes, and role in any given political context."[9] In sum, the constructivist understanding of state identity formation and state interest is inherently linked. In this sense, Alexander Wendt provides a succinct statement of this argument when he writes that "identities are the basis of interests."[10]

In the absence of a dominant theoretical paradigm to guide our understanding of the enlargement of SAARC, we can take the initiative to drive our analysis using constructivist analyses relating to the formal and informal components of organizational membership and norms. Theorizing about EU enlargement, for instance, Frank Schimmelfennig and Ulrich Sedelmeier suggest that it is useful to "concentrate on *formal* and purposive acts of horizontal institutionalization like the conclusion of association agreements or the signing and coming into effect of accession treaties."[11] However, Schimmelfennig and Sedelmeier provide a useful avenue of research by arguing that "organizational norms also spread informally ('diffuse') beyond the boundaries of the organization, both to aspiring members and to states that have no intention of joining."[12]

The constructivist approach to the understanding of state identity formation and the building of identity implies that radical changes in identity can bring about important structural changes in international relations, even in a context of systemic anarchy. To quote Wendt, "given that the structure of an internalized culture and the collective identities of its agents are mutually constitutive, a change in the one implies a change in the other."[13] Based on this premise, constructivist approaches could provide a helpful theoretical framework from which to understand the type of likely structural change that the enlargement of SAARC and the role of external observers entails.[14]

## Country specificity: Afghanistan joins SAARC

One of the most important challenges faced by SAARC has been the proposed enlargement of the association beyond its seven founding members. Since its inception in 1985, only one country has successfully expanded the membership of the association. In November 2005, the government of Afghanistan formally requested to join SAARC. Unsurprisingly, the inclusion of an additional member generated a great deal of public debate, not least because there is uncertainty about the expected benefit of adding a precarious, unstable state to a regional cooperation framework. Moreover, the inclusion of Afghanistan also raised questions about the notion of the malleability of a South Asian identity.

Afghanistan's formal proposal in 2005 to join SAARC, however, highlighted regional differences on the importance of Afghanistan. In an evaluation of the potential expansion of SAARC and its impact on institutional capacity building, O. P. Shah noted that, on the one hand, there was a viewpoint "that the inclusion of Afghanistan into SAARC would open a new window of opportunity for SAARC's resilience and further innovation towards additional avenues for sub-regional co-operation as well as engineering inter-regional co-operation."[15] On the other hand, though, Shah also observed that the potential inclusion of Afghanistan into SAARC raised some doubts given that the country's "main focus is on domestic stabilization and reconstruction."[16] Afghanistan had not yet held its first post-Taliban parliamentary election and there was a great deal of uncertainty about the potential outcome of the Wolesi Jirga (House of the People) election. Another commentator, Shamina Nasreen, also suggested that Afghanistan itself had not fully prepared to join SAARC in 2005. According to her, "one of the reasons could be that SAARC membership may not be cost effective at a time when its main focus was on domestic stabilization and reconstruction."[17] However, the United States viewed Afghanistan's membership of SAARC favorably, principally as a signal that Afghanistan was prepared to engage politically in international organizations. Moreover, as Nasreen argued, "after the election economic benefits are a strong driving force for the country to be included in this organization."[18]

After some initial reluctance and considerable internal debates, the inclusion of Afghanistan as the eighth member of SAARC was announced during the 13th SAARC summit held in Dhaka, Bangladesh, on 12–13 November 2005. In an interview, the Indian prime minister Manmohan Singh declared that "we have agreed to admit Afghanistan as a member of the SAARC."[19] Bangladesh's prime minister Begum Khaleda Zia declared that she "was happy to announce that the SAARC leaders have admitted Afghanistan as a full member of SAARC, subject to completion of formalities."[20] Manmohan Singh also commented favorably on the inclusion of Afghanistan in SAARC. He emphasized that "this is an appropriate recognition of the long-standing ties of culture and history that Afghanistan shares with us."[21] Following the conclusion of the 13th SAARC summit, the SAARC Standing Committee prepared the modalities for the formal acceptance of Afghanistan at its meeting in April 2006, largely to enable Afghanistan to develop a mechanism to induct a new member without having to alter the SAARC Charter. Subsequently, officials from the government of Afghanistan were invited to attend SAARC meetings and the draft modalities were finalized at the 27th SAARC Council of Ministers' meeting held on 31 July–2 August 2006 in Dhaka. Eventually, Afghanistan was formally inducted into the association's declaration, agreements, and legal documents, during the 14th SAARC summit held in Delhi, India, on 3–4 April 2007.

Despite the initial hesitation to admit Afghanistan as a member of SAARC, it is clear that the country has important bonds with the rest of South Asia. Historically, Afghanistan has had strong cultural and commercial links to the South Asian subcontinent, exemplified by the Silk Routes linking Bactra, Begram, Taxila, and Mathura starting from 1 BCE. On the other hand, it is also worth noting that Afghanistan's historical links to South Asia have been borne out of conflict. In the sixteenth century, the Timurid conqueror Zāhir ud-Dīn Muhammad or Babar, the ruler of Farghana, launched a series of attacks from his kingdom's strongholds in Kandahar and defeated the Sultan of Delhi, Ibrahim Lodi, in the first battle of Panipat (1526). On seizing Delhi, Babur founded the Mughal empire. Babur's grandson, Akbar—arguably the greatest of Mughal emperors—consolidated Mughal rule and established an administrative and judicial system that stretched from Afghanistan to present-day Bangladesh. On the basis of these historical antecedents, Afghanistan's links to contemporary South Asia carry a great deal of resonance.[22]

Nevertheless, when considering the incorporation of Afghanistan in SAARC one cannot overlook the fact that the historical connection between Afghanistan and the rest of South Asia has not been consistently maintained. As a result of overarching imperatives, there has been a gradual delinking of Afghanistan from the subcontinent. The German biogeographer Alexander von Humboldt is credited with conceiving a distinct geographic region, namely Central Asia, which bundled Afghanistan with other Turkic-speaking nomadic peoples into one cohesive geographic unit.[23] The cultural historian, Friedrich von Hellwald, later defined Central Asia on the basis of shared linguistic and cultural characteristics. In his view, there was a cultural coherence of the region comprising the Altai region, the Kazakh plains, Zhetysu, Dzungaria, Tian Shan, including Afghanistan and regions of India.[24]

The geographic distinctiveness of Afghanistan began to emerge and was reinforced following the destruction of Elphinstone's army during the first Anglo-Afghan war (1839–42) and the turbulent governance of that country in the nineteenth century. During the period of consolidation of British colonial rule in British India, particularly during the rule of Viceroy Sir John Lawrence (1864–9), Afghanistan gradually began to be perceived as standing outside the parameters of South Asia, namely in Central Asia. Afghanistan's attainment of complete independence from Britain after the third Anglo-Afghan war (1919)—decades before India's independence from Britain in 1947—further isolated Afghanistan from the rest of South Asia.

As we evaluate the enlargement of SAARC, we can see that the inclusion of Afghanistan proved an important challenge to the perception of South Asia as a monolithic region. On the basis of historical antecedents, Afghanistan was culturally inside and outside of South Asia. Afghanistan's placing within SAARC was given careful thought by its president, Hamid Karzai. During the 14th SAARC summit, President Karzai commented on his country as a link between Central Asia and South Asia, though he framed this relationship instrumentally, on the basis of expected trade links. President Karzai argued that "[o]ur vision for Afghanistan and its people is one where we act as a conduit for growing regional trade."[25] In outlining the benefits of Afghanistan joining SAARC, President Karzai also reiterated that SAARC members "will also have greater ease of access to the Central and South Asian markets, and the regions' natural resources which are crucial drivers of economic growth."[26]

## SAARC observers

The issue of SAARC's enlargement is closely linked to the participation of countries and multilateral organizations as SAARC observers. During the summit declaration issued at the 13th SAARC summit, Afghanistan's petition to become a member was formally accepted by the heads of state and government of SAARC member countries. Likewise, the 13th SAARC summit declaration also approved the incorporation of countries, and both regional and international organizations, as SAARC observers. In the summit declaration it was noted that the first two countries to be conditionally granted SAARC observer status would be the People's Republic of China and Japan. However, the summit declaration did not provide a comprehensive understanding of the debate that took place institutionally. The inclusion of China as an observer had been steadfastly rejected by India, specifically during the SAARC council of foreign ministers' meeting held on 11 November 2005. According to Pakistani press reports, India "was the only SAARC member state that strongly opposed the Chinese bid to join the regional alliance" and it apparently "made its position loud and clear on this issue."[27] At the SAARC summit meeting in Dhaka, King Gyanendra of Nepal urged India to reconsider its stance. He suggested that Nepal could provide "a level playing field for both our neighbours to reap the benefits of a promising global economic order."[28] However, India later softened its stance and by the end of the 2005 SAARC summit meeting in Dhaka, the Indian prime minister Manmohan Singh declared that "we also welcome the intent shown by China and Japan to get observer status and this matter will be sorted out in the next few months."[29]

Since SAARC was institutionally not equipped to incorporate new SAARC members or observers, the modalities for granting SAARC observer status were discussed at the 27th Council of Ministers' meeting held in August 2006 in Dhaka. Applications for SAARC observer status from the EU, South Korea, and the United States, were also considered. Eventually, a set of Guidelines for Cooperation with Observers was adopted at the 15th SAARC summit held in Colombo, Sri Lanka, in 2008. As Box 2.1 shows, the number of SAARC observers has increased rapidly. Since the 2005 SAARC summit, up to eight countries and one

***Box 2.1* SAARC observers (date of joining)**

- China (2005)
- Japan (2005)
- European Union (2006)
- South Korea (2006)
- United States of America (2006)
- Mauritius (2007)
- Iran (2008)
- Australia (2008)
- Myanmar (Burma) (2008)

Source: Extracted from the South Asian Association for Regional Cooperation website (available at: www.saarc-sec.org/Cooperation-with-Observers/13).

international organization have been granted SAARC observer status. At present, the nine SAARC observers are Australia, China, the European Union, Iran, Japan, Mauritius, Myanmar (Burma), South Korea, and the United States.

The level of interest and motivation for participating in SAARC as an observer varies, but there is a general acceptance that South Asia is an important economic and political hub. For instance, Japan's Ministry of Foreign Affairs notes that it views SAARC "as an association significant for its ability to provide a platform for the stability and development of the South Asia region."[30] In Japan's case, the primary motivation for engaging with SAARC lies in its support for democracy and peace-building, the promotion of regional connectivity, and person-to-person exchanges.[31] In official statements, Australia has also reiterated the benefit of engaging with SAARC in order to enhance closer ties with individual SAARC nations on the issues of trade, education, science and technology cooperation, and counter-terrorism.[32]

Some commentators on SAARC suggest that the involvement of a growing number of SAARC observers represents both challenges and opportunities for the sustainability of the association. According to Rashid Ahmad Khan, "while it enhances the international stature of SAARC and creates strong imperatives for peace and cooperation, it can boost foreign direct investment, open up transit trade facilities, provide connectivity and promote inter-regional trade and economic cooperation opportunities among the member states."[33] At the same time, though, involvement by too many international observers can alter—and even distort—the core functions of the institution. In the concrete case of SAARC, the growth of international observers with conflicting policy agendas could dilute the objective of promoting intraregional cooperation. Based on this assumption, Khan cautions that "while the expansion of SAARC through the inclusion of new members and observers might contribute to the growth of economic cooperation among the member states and the organization, it can also lead to new power games in South Asia as states with divergent political agendas register their presence and pursue their strategic objectives in the SAARC."[34]

Within the context of a debate on the impact of international observers, one of the most intriguing developments relating to the composition of SAARC has been the request by several observer states to become fully fledged members of SAARC. China, for instance, has been gradually expressing its interest in enhancing its involvement with SAARC. In 1996, during an official visit to Pakistan, the Chinese president Jiang Zemin commented favorably on the role of SAARC in promoting regional stability. Jiang Zemin argued that "we are pleased to see the heartening progress made by the South Asian countries in recent years in improving their relations with one another and strengthening regional cooperation. The South Asian Association for Regional Cooperation (SAARC) has played a meaningful role in promoting peace, stability and economic cooperation in the region."[35]

Subsequent statements issued by China's leaders and Ministry of Foreign Affairs have pinpointed the country's interest in participating in multilateral arrangements to enhance cooperation in South Asia. Initially, these expressions of involvement took the form of ministerial-level joint communiqués with selected South Asian countries. The initial basis of Chinese involvement in collaboration revolved around strengthening the cooperation agreement between the China Council for the Promotion of International Trade (CCPIT) and the SAARC Chamber of Commerce and Industry (SCCI) in Kunming, China.[36] Eventually, the declarations of expected involvement have become more direct. Thus, on 27 March 2007, the spokesman for the Chinese Ministry of Foreign Affairs commented that "SAARC is an important regional cooperation organization in South Asia. China has been following and supporting the cooperation process of SAARC. Not long ago, China was accepted as an observer of SAARC and we welcome that. As a friendly neighbour of South Asia, we are ready to conduct exchanges and cooperation with SAARC in light of the principle of equality, mutual benefit, and win-win cooperation with a view to making positive contributions to the cooperation, development and prosperity of South Asia."[37] A week later, during Chinese foreign minister Li Zhaoxing's participation at the 14th SAARC summit, Minister Li commented that China's interest in engaging with SAARC was crucial because "the fundamental objective of China's policy towards South Asia is stability, development and good neighbourly relations."[38] A year later, during the official ceremonies marking the start of the 2008 Olympic Games, President Hu Jintao declared that "China is ready to conduct equal dialogue and pragmatic cooperation with SAARC based on the spirit of equality, mutual trust and win-win cooperation and play a constructive role in pushing forward the SAARC cooperation process."[39]

The recent calibration of China's interest in South Asia and SAARC has been framed from the point of view of a shared cultural heritage. The conception that China has long-standing cultural relations with South Asia has been particularly emphasized by government-sponsored Chinese think tanks. For instance, citing a report issued by the Chinese Academy of Social Sciences (CASS), He Hailin observes that "the interactions between China and South Asia could date back to [the] 3rd century BC."[40] Nevertheless, it is also obvious that cultural links alone are not likely to sustain a strong partnership and that strategic and economic considerations have also played a part in China's interest in the region.[41] China fought a border war with India in 1962 and the relationship has been animated by a lingering diplomatic dispute about the exact territorial claims being made by India and China. Traditionally, China has also enjoyed a strategic partnership with Pakistan, India's traditional enemy. More recently, China has strengthened bilateral relations with other South Asian countries, notably Sri Lanka, Bangladesh, and Nepal.

The prospect of improved trade relations has also been a critical driver in China's interest in SAARC. As Lawrence Sáez and Crystal Chang have noted, as recently as 2007, China's exports to all South Asian countries amounted to 8.7 percent of China's exports to Asian countries and just 2.8 percent of China's exports globally.[42] Chinese think tank commentators on China's commercial interests in South Asia have begun to view SAARC as a potential instrument to enhance Chinese engagement in South Asia. Zhang Yunling, another analyst from CASS, has noted that China and South Asia "have developed their economic relations under a regional framework. For instance, China became an observer of SAARC, which provides a venue to discuss the trade and investment facilitation programs, among others."[43] To this effect, the Chinese government has been keen to follow the development of a SAARC-initiated free trade area (FTA) and its potential impact on growing Chinese exports to South Asia.

However, Chinese engagement with South Asia, via the SAARC, is realistic and pragmatic. While praising the SAARC-initiated free trade area, Zhang Yunling has hypothesized that "political inertia could slow down the SAARC FTA process" and concluded that "China should explore other avenues to enhance its integration with the region."[44] Another CASS commentator, Lu Jianren, has been more pessimistic about the levels of economic integration in South Asia, particularly on the basis of SAARC sponsorship. He has written that "in South Asia, the South Asian Association for Regional Cooperation (SAARC) was set up in 1985, but its economic cooperation process is slow and at a low level."[45]

China's interest in conducting an equal dialogue and pragmatic cooperation with SAARC has been replicated by other SAARC observers, albeit in a more belated, unstructured, and ineffective manner. In 2008, for instance, Myanmar (Burma) also requested an application for full membership to SAARC.[46] Iran has also indicated an interest in becoming a member of SAARC with foreign minister Kamal Kharazzi announcing in February 2005 that the country had long studied the possibility of accession to SAARC.[47] Subsequent Iranian foreign ministers have continued to reiterate Iran's interest in joining SAARC. While stressing the growing trade relations between Iran and South Asia, Iranian foreign minister Manouchehr Mottaki highlighted the historical ties that link Iran and South Asia.[48] Until recently, though, Iranian declarations of interest to join SAARC have not been framed in more concrete actions.

Myanmar's unconvincing bid to become a SAARC member failed, but China and Iran attempted to join SAARC in 2010 using a rather understated approach. On the occasion of the 16th SAARC summit, held in Thimpu, Bhutan, in April 2010, China and Iran formally attempted to have their membership request incorporated into the summit's agenda and SAARC Secretary General Sheel Kant Sharma had agreed that such a request would be incorporated into the agenda. However, China and Iran's request was sharply rejected by New Delhi. As the date of the 16th SAARC summit drew closer, the SAARC secretary general announced that the request by India and Iran would not be included in the agenda because "SAARC has failed to take up a significant pace, the membership will not be extended."[49] A week later, India's foreign secretary, Nirupama Rao, commented on the proposed expansion of SAARC membership and without acknowledging any explicit opposition to China and Iran's membership bid she said: "A fresh entry into SAARC? I am afraid not. We have eight members and that is the way it is going to stay."[50]

Clearly, the incorporation of China as a SAARC member state would not only represent a major change in the internal dynamics of the association but would also be viewed as a threat in Indian government circles. Moreover, the rapid growth in the number of institutions that enjoy SAARC observer status has also altered the expectation that the association should have a strictly regional focus. To that effect, SAARC now seeks to provide greater clarity regarding the expected role of SAARC observers. During the 15th SAARC summit, SAARC member states agreed to approve a set of Guidelines for Cooperation with Observers and pledged to look "forward to working with them in the common pursuit of the partnership for growth for our people."[51]

The guidelines included the provision that SAARC observers pledge to subscribe to the tenets outlined in the SAARC Charter and objectives. Procedurally, the guidelines enable a SAARC observer country to attend the opening and closing sessions of a SAARC summit. A provision with similar scope also gives SAARC observers limited participation at SAARC Council of Ministers' meetings and other SAARC-related ministerial meetings. On the other hand the guidelines circumscribe the participation of SAARC observers at SAARC summits. According to the guidelines, SAARC observers are not allowed to make any statements about areas of concern during a SAARC meeting or summit; however, they are able to circulate them. In addition, SAARC observers are permitted to make proposals regarding cooperation and joint venture projects with the approval of the relevant SAARC committees. Nevertheless, one of the key features of the guidelines was to put a moratorium on the admission of new observers.

## SAARC's relations with intergovernmental organizations

SAARC enjoys engagement with a number of intergovernmental organizations. Between 1993 and 2010, SAARC signed 23 Memorandums of Understanding (MoUs) with various intergovernmental organizations. The first MoU of this type was signed with two UN agencies, the United Nations Conference on Trade and Development (UNCTAD) and the United Nations Children's Fund (UNICEF).[52] Subsequently, SAARC has signed additional MoUs with a host of other UN agencies, including the United Nations Economic and Social Commission (UNESCAP, 1994), the United Nations Development Program (UNDP, 1995), the United Nations Office on Drugs and Crime (UNODC, 1995), the United Nations Fund for Women (UNIFEM, 2001), the Joint United Nations Program on HIV/AIDS (UNAIDS, 2004), the United Nations Environment Program (UNEP, 2007), the United Nations International Strategy for Disaster Reduction (UN/ISDR, 2008), and the United Nations Educational, Scientific, and Cultural Organization (UNESCO, 2008).[53]

As the substantial number of MoUs signed shows, it is clear that SAARC believes that the association has an affinity with the UN and its leading agencies. Likewise, it has signed MoUs with the International Telecommunications Union (ITU, 1997), the World Health Organization (WHO, 2000), the World Bank (WB, 2004), and the Food and Agriculture Organization (FAO, 2004).[54] Nevertheless, it is difficult to point to any specific initiative that has emerged on the basis of SAARC MoUs with intergovernmental institutions.

Given its focus on developmental issues, SAARC has also engaged with national and regional developmental and environmental agencies. To that effect, SAARC has signed MoUs with Asia Pacific Telecommunity (APT, 1994), the Canadian International Development Agency (CIDA, 1997), the Physikalisch-Technische Bundesanstalt (PTB, 2003), South Asia Cooperative Environment Program (SACEP, 2004), the Asian Development Bank (ADB, 2004), the Japan Special Fund (JSF, 2006), the Asian Disaster Preparedness Center (ADPC, 2006), and the Center on Integrated Rural Development for Asia and the Pacific (CIRDAP, 2007). SAARC also developed collaborative arrangements with a number of organizations without signing a MoU. These include arrangements with the ASEAN, the German Society for Technical Cooperation (Deutsche Gesellschaft für Technische Zusammenarbeit, GTZ), the United Nations Industrial Development Organization (UNIDO), and the International Standards Organization (ISO).

Given the large number of MoUs that SAARC has signed with intergovernmental organizations and collaboration agreements (without a MoU), one may be tempted to conclude that the aggregate effect of these agreements has been rather limited. Although most of the MoUs signed by SAARC have merely remained an expression of interest in collaboration, one can only hope that in the future there may be concrete collaborative outcomes between SAARC and other like-minded institutions.[55]

In the case of the European Commission, however, it appears that the signing of a MoU in 1996 should have heralded the deepening of its relationship with the association. The Commission became a SAARC observer in 2006. From the EU's perspective, cooperation between the European Commission and SAARC "should notably seek to promote the harmonisation of standards; facilitate trade; raise awareness about the benefits of regional cooperation; and promote business networking in the SAARC area."[56] Carried to their full potential, cooperation between SAARC and the EU should be mutually beneficial. Nevertheless, independent analyses of the trends in EU-SAARC relations offer a more pessimistic assessment. Other than the inclusion of SAARC in the EU's generalized system of preferences (GSP) cumulative clause of the rules of origin, Rajendra Jain observes wryly that "there has been very limited cooperation between the European Union and SAARC."[57] As

Jain points out, logistical problems within the operation of the EU and SAARC, respectively, have prevented the implementation of any collaborative initiatives. In a more critical assessment, though, Christopher Piening argues that the inability of India and Pakistan to cooperate makes SAARC "unsuitable as a dialogue partner."[58]

## The enlargement of SAARC and the question of identity

The question of the enlargement of SAARC and, by logical implication, the confusion that has emerged over the proposed role of external observers as discussed in this chapter cannot be detached from important debates in international relations theory. On one hand, the debates that preceded the inclusion of Afghanistan in SAARC or the controversy surrounding Iran or China's applications for SAARC membership could be explained if we understand state action on the basis of competitive power politics, in the absence of a central authority in an international system. On the other hand, such controversies can be seen as a procedure, wherein states are attempting to adapt to changing conceptions of interest.

Neorealist and neoliberal institutionalist approaches tend to offer systemic explanations of state action. In contrast, a constructivist approach to international relations assumes the centrality of national identity in the construction of national interest. In Alexander Wendt's words this amounts to a consideration of "their own identities and interests, which reflect beliefs about who they are in such situations; and what they think others will do, which reflect beliefs about identities and interests."[59] In this sense, Wendt offers a useful theoretical dichotomy on how to view the influences that shape state action. Wendt argues that state action can be interpreted to be "influenced by 'structure' (anarchy and the distribution of power) versus 'process' (interaction and learning) and institutions."[60]

Based on these assumptions, Wendt and other constructivists have attempted to develop an evolutionary model of identity formation, wherein "identities are produced and reproduced in the social process."[61] In this conceptualization of the international system, structural change is possible provided that collective identity formation is present. Building on this work, there have been some constructivist approaches to regionalism and region-building, notably developing a school of thought that has been termed the "new regionalism." Neumann, Hettne, Bøås, Marchand, and Shaw, among others, have attempted to explore the role that regions have played in an emerging world order characterized by economic interdependence.[62] In this context, Hettne writes of a regional community that can be defined whenever "an enduring organizational framework (formal or less formal) facilitates and promotes social communication and convergence of values and actions through the region, creating a transnational civil society, characterized by social trust also at the regional level."[63]

The analysis of regional rivalry and cooperation in South Asia, using constructivist assumptions, is somewhat sparse but has an excellent pedigree. Taking South Asia as an empirical example, Barry Buzan and Gowher Rizvi developed the building blocks for a framework of regional security analysis. Buzan argued that regional security systems can be defined in terms of patterns of amity and enmity and are "substantially confined within some particular geographical area."[64] In Buzan's view, the chief characteristic of a regional security complex is that it rests "on the interdependence of rivalry rather than on the interdependence of shared interests."[65] Buzan and Rizvi maintained that, despite evidence of local rivalry, "considerable local stabilities are complemented by some strong communities in the relationship of outside powers to the South Asia region." In their opinion, these external actors "all have durable interests in South Asia which stem more from their concerns about each other than from any intrinsic interest in South Asia."[66] Advocates of the view that South Asia is a regional security complex are cognizant of the fact that an alteration of alliances between external players and individual countries in South Asia could have an impact on local or regional patterns of security relations. However, Buzan and Rizvi hypothesized that "even a transformation of external links on as large a scale as this would not disturb the continuity of the status quo within South Asia, because it would not change the essential structure of relations within the local security complex."[67]

Deepening the constructivist literature on region and identity in South Asia, Sinderpal Singh has also attempted to understand the different processes used to define South Asia as a region, whether they be on the basis of geographic or cultural traits. Singh also argues that South Asia can be defined in geopolitical terms, just as Buzan and Rizvi do when discussing the concept of a South Asian regional security complex. Similarly, regions can be defined on economic terms. In Singh's view, the formation of SAARC is particularly pertinent in this respect because "it signaled the beginning of the attempt to define South Asia on economic foundations."[68]

The constructivist literature on identity formation and region-building is a useful avenue through which to understand the concept of SAARC's enlargement as discussed in this chapter. However, it also raises some inherent limitations in the constructivist literature. If we examine the mini case study of Afghanistan's efforts to become a member of SAARC, we find that a disaggregated understanding of regional identity in the context of South Asia is not particularly illuminating. Writing in the mid-1980s, during the height of the Soviet Union's involvement in Afghanistan, Buzan and Rizvi were torn and argued that Afghanistan "can be seen either as an overlay of part of the South Asian complex, or else as an external transformation of it (i.e., a change in its outer boundary) resulting from the effective annexation of one of its peripheral members by an outside power."[69]

Authors adopting a constructivist approach have also struggled to define whether China forms part of a South Asian region, however configured. Buzan acknowledged that one of the major difficulties in identifying a regional security complex is the existence of a lopsided relationship between the largest states in the region. He used the example of China as a clear example of this puzzle. Buzan argued that "China is a major security concern for India: arguably even the principal one."[70] He then added that these types of situations give rise to two levels of a security complex, a lower and a higher level. In the case of China, Buzan believed that the country exhibits a higher level complex, therefore its "power is sufficient to impinge on several sectors of what their enormous physical size makes a vast 'local environment'."[71] Elsewhere, Buzan hesitated to include China as part of the South Asia region, but then considered that "the remaining possibility is that the South Asian complex will undergo an external transformation on the basis of developments in the relations between India and China."[72]

Other authors have been more explicit in their rejection of additional countries being included in the region of South Asia, primarily because their links to the area are too tenuous. For instance, Sinderpal Singh argued that "China and Burma are not part of this 'region' on geographical, cultural, economic or even geopolitical grounds." Writing years before Afghanistan became a full SAARC member, Singh also maintained that Afghanistan "while sharing a much weaker consensus in the literature, is still typically thought to be marginal to the 'natural' region of South Asia."[73]

## Conclusion

The enlargement of SAARC, with the inclusion of Afghanistan, demonstrates that the landscape of South Asia can be malleable. It is not inconceivable that at some stage a country with strong historical roots in the rest of the Indian subcontinent, like Myanmar or even Mauritius, could also form part of SAARC. The controversy surrounding the inclusion of Afghanistan in SAARC put into question the proposition that the association could not be defined along broader parameters. Some countries outside of South Asia enjoy observer status with SAARC. However, the expression of interest by one of these countries (i.e., China) to formally join SAARC as a constituent member state has rattled the institutional identity of the association. Should there ever be a possibility that the citizens of countries in South Asia develop a strong sense of collective identity (as South Asians), such a prospect would be severely weakened.

The example of the internal debate occurring in the EU about the proposed accession of Turkey to the Union shows how the limits of what constitutes a meaningful community are being tested. In other words, the incorporation of a member state that does not appear to share similar socio-cultural attributes of the other member states reveals inherent fears within the overall association. The inclusion of China in SAARC would indelibly alter the implicit regional hegemonic status that India enjoys in South Asia. In China's case, though, it is unlikely that it will ever join the association formally. Its participation, though, is likely to acquire a unique status, equivalent to the special relationship that some countries enjoy vis-à-vis ASEAN.[74] In due course, we may start to refer to SAARC + 3.

Ironically, while potentially destroying the emerging prominence that SAARC gives to the different countries in South Asia, it is conceivable that the inclusion of China as a SAARC member state could make the association a much more effective and focused regional organization. In recent decades, China has been keen to assert its power in international organizations. More importantly, the country has viewed regional organizations as instruments of its own foreign policy. For instance, China's assertiveness within the framework of the SCO suggests that eagerness on the part of China to provide leadership can have the consequence of revitalizing an otherwise dormant and unfocused regional organization. In sharp contrast to China's keenness to join SAARC, India has, thus far, been reluctant to unilaterally assert its leadership in an international setting. For instance, India has been a reluctant participant in the SCO, an association within which it enjoys observer status. It could be argued that in this particular case, India has been a reluctant observer, often being represented by mid-level diplomats. India's unwillingness to be viewed as a global leader is evidenced by its participation in other institutions.

The development of a South Asian regional identity, if conceived from a norms-based constructivist approach, suggests that identity and its constitutive behaviors are tracing, historically contingent, limiting and defining. Constructivism contends that domestic identity is important in international relations; therefore, security is not merely derived from international sources, but the influence of domestic actors is important. As such, national security and foreign policy are evolutionary processes based on learning.

In my view, a constructivist approach to strategic culture in South Asia could be a useful departure point from which to understand the debates surrounding the inclusion of Afghanistan as a member of SAARC as well as the association's confusion about how to incorporate external actors as SAARC observers. As we will examine in the next chapter, South Asia's changing security environment operates within a context in which India plays a dominant role. Nevertheless, India has traditionally been hesitant to exercise its dominance regionally. However, some regional actors in South Asia regard India as a hegemonic actor, rather than as a regional leader. As we attempt to understand the reasons for the limited success of SAARC in promoting regional cooperation on security, economics and other issues, it may be useful to reframe this understanding through a norms-based approach such as that offered by constructivists.

# 3 Security and economic cooperation

- Realism and regionalism in SAARC
- Military and strategic cooperation
- Economic cooperation
- Conclusion

Much of the extant literature on South Asia's regional cooperation has converged on the perceived lack of effectiveness of SAARC. For instance, Kishore Dash offers a voice to this perspective when he writes that "to some, SAARC is merely a talking shop, which can provide nothing more than a lip service to the various issues of peace and development in the region."[1] Despite its shortcomings, however, Dash has argued that although SAARC "may not be a panacea to the region's problems, but its existence has certainly provided an opportunity for the policy makers, administrators, and experts to meet regularly and hold informal dialogues on important bilateral and regional issues."[2] Thus, the strongest defense of SAARC is that it provides an informal forum for the mediation of important regional cooperation challenges. Even S. D. Muni suggests that without SAARC, "the deterioration in the regional strategic environment would have been greater and moved faster."[3]

In this chapter I will show the types of important improvements in regional security and economic cooperation that have taken place in South Asia, which have been mediated by SAARC. Special attention will be paid to the ratification of the SAARC Preferential Trading Arrangement (SAPTA) in December 1995, arguably one of SAARC's most important achievements since its inception. As we shall discuss in this chapter, however, we should acknowledge the differing perspectives presented regarding the effectiveness of SAARC, as the literature on regional cooperation in South Asia has not successfully directly tackled the challenges posed by neorealist critiques of international organizations.

## Realism and regionalism in SAARC

Any analysis of regional cooperation institutions, like SAARC, has to face the challenges posed by the neorealist literature on the effectiveness of international institutions. One of the key challenges in designing an international institution is the threat that the institution may prove ineffective. Many observers of SAARC instinctively lament the perceived lack of impact of the association. As some neorealist scholars have argued, a secondary challenge to institutions is the potential effect that an ineffective international organization may have. According to Giulio Gallarotti, a poorly managed organization can in addition destabilize the international system "when its solutions discourage from pursuing more substantive or long-term resolutions to international problems, including disputes, or when it serves as a substitute for responsible domestic or foreign policy."[4]

Another key neorealist challenge to the success of an international organization is the possibility that the institution may not be able to encourage cooperation on a wide range of critical issues. Based on the assumption that states operate in a state of relentless security competition, the neorealist literature on international institutions eschews the possibility that to promote stability states can cooperate on critical issues. For instance, John Mearsheimer's central conclusion in assessing the importance of international institutions was that "institutions hold little promise for promoting stability in the post-Cold War world."[5] Within the neorealist framework, states can be expected to cooperate, but such behavior is inhibited by the expectation that states seek relative gains and share a concern about cheating by rival states. In this sense, Mearsheimer concludes that whatever level of cooperation through institutions takes place, it is in the anticipation that "those rules reflect state calculations of self-interest based primarily on the international distribution of power."[6]

Other neorealist interpretations of the process of regional integration give primacy to the view that the pace, direction, and institutional rule trajectories of regional integration are determinative of the initiation and trajectory of the integration process. However, using the example of the European monetary union, Joseph Grieco suggests that neorealism can adopt an amended view of the significance of international institutions via what he terms a "voice opportunities thesis."[7] In an amended neorealist perspective on the value of institutions, states evaluate an existing or prospective collaborative endeavor provided that the rules establishing such a framework supply them with specific benefits. Among the expected benefits from collaborative engagement, Grieco lists "increased diversity of consumption, opportunities, enhanced efficiency of production, and greater national income resulting from mutual reductions in trade barriers … the level of policy influence partners have or might attain in the collaborative arrangement."[8]

Neoliberal institutionalist, functionalist, and structural interdependence approaches in international relations theory have provided a range of counterpoints to the oversimplified vision of the international system provided by neorealist thinking. One key departure from neorealism revolves around the assumption of the centrality of state-society relations.[9] In the neoliberal institutionalist perspective, regional integration schemes develop for the purpose of monitoring and enforcing agreements between states.[10] In this sense, states voluntarily delegate some of their authority to supranational institutions, provided that there is close monitoring of this transfer of authority. Functionalist approaches also stress the proposition, as argued by Ernst Haas, that "political integration is the process whereby actors shift their loyalties, expectations, and political activities toward a new center, whose institutions possess or demand jurisdiction over preexisting national states."[11] From this perspective, there is a reciprocal institutional feedback, whereby international institutions are capable of changing their members' preferences. In Haas' words, there is "progressive penetration from supranational institutions into the lower reaches of decision-making at the national level."[12]

From a theoretical perspective, a holistic approach to the success of regional institutions includes a number of issues. According to Werner Feld and Gavin Boyd, other factors included in the literature include similarities of regional configuration, political sociology, political culture, political psychology, authority structures and influence patterns, regional institutions, regional foreign policy behavior, interdependencies, regional cooperation and conflict between members, and affinity in developmental issues.[13] Moreover, critiques of the relative importance of institutions in a regional context have also emerged from the institutionalist and integration theory literature. Notably, Ernst Haas' later missive on the importance of regional integration theory suggests that regionalism faces additional challenges.[14]

Some authors, focusing on SAARC, have pointed out the institutional peculiarities of the association. According to S. D. Muni, one of the academic doyens on the subject of India's foreign policy, unlike other similar enterprises SAARC is "characterized by political disharmony and strategic schism."[15] In Muni's view, the push toward greater South Asian cooperation mediated through SAARC has gone hand in hand with a widening strategic divide in the region, particularly between India and Pakistan.

In a study of SAARC, Iftekharuzzaman argued that the basic prerequisites for the success of regional cooperation included convergence on security perceptions, commonalities of political and ideological orientations, common foreign policy orientations (given the context of regional asymmetry), and consensus on the role of the pivotal power in the region (i.e., India).[16] Other critics of SAARC, such as Muhammed Shamshul Huq, have also seized on the issue of regional asymmetry. In a detailed and perceptive evaluation of the prospects for SAARC, Huq asked that "even if the fact of asymmetry and lack of economic complementarity is overlooked, how can the member-states expect to overcome the barrier of great divergence in their security perceptions rooted in their historical memories of discord, and conflicts further accelerated by the wide disparity in their military strength?"[17] In writing about obstacles to economic cooperation in the economic sphere, Govind Agrawal also highlights the impact of asymmetry and notes that "incongruence of economic interests resulting from disparities and disadvantages of size, population, location and levels of economic development, pose serious obstacles to harmonious regional cooperation."[18]

## Military and strategic cooperation

The steps undertaken in the late 1970s leading to the creation of SAARC took place within the context of two important developments in the region. The December 1979 invasion of Afghanistan prompted a swift strategic realignment in the region. From the point of view of the United States, the invasion of Afghanistan helped the Soviet Union to consolidate a strategic position near the Persian Gulf and the Indian Ocean which threatened the free supply of oil from the Middle East. In light of the emerging Iranian revolution, the proximity of Pakistan to Afghanistan immediately made Pakistan an invaluable front-line state against the Soviet Union. Reacting to this threat, US president Jimmy Carter outlined a strategic vision—later dubbed the Carter Doctrine—in his third State of the Union address. Even though the Carter administration had been critical of the violations of human rights taking place in Pakistan during the initial years of President Zia-ul-Haq's rule, Carter pledged to reconfirm the 1959 agreement "to help Pakistan preserve its independence and its integrity."[19] He also stressed that the United States was working with other countries in the region "to share a cooperative security framework that respects differing values and political beliefs, yet which enhances the independence, security, and prosperity of all."[20]

President Carter viewed South Asia as an important region and his visit in 1978 to India was much heralded. However, the rapidly changing

US strategic imperative in the region prompted President Carter to encourage leaders in South Asia to develop a more regionally focused agenda to settle their prevailing disputes. According to S. D. Muni, President Carter "sent high level emissaries to India and Pakistan to explain this framework and persuade the antagonistic neighbors to 'evolve a regional approach' toward the 'fundamentally changed situation' in the region."[21] Nevertheless, some analysts have presented Carter's interest in South Asia as suggesting the broader scope of the Carter Doctrine, namely the development of a "third strategic zone" to counteract a potential "arc of crisis" in the Gulf area.[22] Some analysts have pointed to the establishment of the Rapid Deployment Force (later renamed U.S. Central Command, CENTCOM) as evidence that South Asia—particularly Pakistan—was considered essential within the US security umbrella.[23]

Whatever their inherent motivation, though, Carter's entreaties for a new cooperative security framework in Southwest and South Asia were not shared by India, particularly once Indira Gandhi was restored to power as prime minister after the 1980 general election in India. Indira Gandhi reaffirmed India's stance of non-alignment and refused to condemn the Soviet invasion of Afghanistan explicitly, instead calling for a withdrawal of all foreign forces from Afghanistan. However, India's impartiality on this subject was in question in light of the fact that Indira Gandhi had enthusiastically signed the 1971 Indo-Soviet Treaty of Peace, Friendship and Cooperation, an agreement that had an enormous impact on India's ability to acquire military hardware.

From the point of view of the United States, the Soviet invasion of Afghanistan drove a further strategic wedge between Pakistan and India. In contrast, the growing interest among South Asia's leaders to create a regional cooperation organization had to sidestep from taking a concerted stance on the issue of Afghanistan and instead converged on an explicitly regional strategic issue, namely the sharing of river water. In May 1980, President Zia of Bangladesh proposed a regional summit to address these concerns and drafted a proposal. According to S. D. Muni, the Bangladeshi proposal suggested by President Zia was "drastically reformulated" and instead "a South Asian consensus emerged in favor of building regional cooperation from below, without much political fanfare and through the establishment of cooperative linkages in those areas seen as beneficial by all the seven states of the region and in which no controversies are involved."[24] In sum, SAARC emerged from a strategic context in which the regional actors had very distinct internal and external perceptions of threat.

A traditional approach to security in South Asia can be expressed in terms of larger systemic forces, particularly drawing upon India's dominant role in the region. The issue of India's increased influence in the region figures prominently in Barry Buzan's conceptualization of a regional security complex in South Asia. In Buzan's view, India's neighbors are inherently tied into a security complex with India, primarily due to their close social, political and economic links. However, by virtue of the bilateral economic relations between India and its neighbors, Buzan notes that SAARC "does not affect the security politics of the region in any way."[25] Buzan then adds that "if India can sustain its recent levels of economic growth, and if regional trade increases either through bilateral agreements, or by the realization of the South Asia Free Trade Area slated for 2005, then India's emergent hegemony will increase."[26]

There is a clash of views, ranging from Nehru's influence on the conceptualization of Indian foreign policy, to a more regionally focused foreign policy strategy proposed by Bangladesh, Nepal, or even Pakistan. In an insightful analysis of India's strategic self-perception, Subrata Mitra argued that "the hiatus between India's self-perception as a status quo power and its perception by the neighbouring states as a regional bully is the main cause of stalemate in the South Asian security environment."[27]

A constructivist approach to the understanding of security focuses instead on the cultural and historical transmission of norms, beliefs, and values pertinent to the security policy and outlook of the state. From the constructivist viewpoint, the development of norms overrides key episodes, such as the end of the Cold War or 9/11. However, the constructivist literature on region-building on the basis of identity and norm-building among the actors faces challenges from the conventional idea of region-building whereby India would be seen as the dominant actor in South Asia. In this situation, India's inherent dominance would diminish the notion of South Asian identity.

The security perceptions of different SAARC members are also linked to their internal domestic capabilities. If one examines the military capabilities of the different actors in South Asia, it is not surprising to note that there is an inherent regional asymmetry. Table 3.1 illustrates the basic conventional force capabilities of the SAARC member states.

As Table 3.1 shows, the distance between India's military capabilities in conventional terms vis-à-vis other SAARC members is considerable. Nearly 60 percent of total armed forces in South Asia are from India. Pakistan, India's principal contiguous military adversary, has larger military expenditures (relative to gross domestic product) than any other member of SAARC.[28] However, nearly 80 percent of nominal military expenditures made in South Asia come from India.

*Table 3.1* Comparative data on conventional armed force capabilities and military expenditures in South Asia in 1985, 1995, and 2005

*1985*

| | *Afghanistan* | *Bangladesh* | *India* | *Nepal* | *Pakistan* | *Sri Lanka* |
|---|---|---|---|---|---|---|
| Total Armed Forces | 47,000 | 91,300 | 1,260,000 | 25,000 | 482,800 | 37,660 |
| Army | 40,000 | 81,800 | 1,100,000 | 25,000 | 450,000 | 30,000 |
| Air Force | 7,000 | 3,000 | 113,000 | n.a. | 17,600 | 3,700 |
| Navy | n.a. | 6,500 | 47,000 | n.a. | 15,200 | 3,960 |
| Military expenditure (in $ millions)* | n.a. | 412 | 14,141 | 52 | 3,419 | 414 |
| Military expenditure (as a % of GDP) | n.a. | 1 | 3.6 | 0.9 | 6.2 | 2.4 |

*1995*

| | *Afghanistan* | *Bangladesh* | *India* | *Nepal* | *Pakistan* | *Sri Lanka* |
|---|---|---|---|---|---|---|
| Total Armed Forces | n.a. | 115,500 | 1,145,000 | 35,000 | 587,000 | 125,300 |
| Army | n.a. | 101,000 | 980,000 | 34,800 | 520,000 | 105,000 |
| Air Force | n.a. | 6,500 | 110,000 | 200 | 45,000 | 10,000 |
| Navy | n.a. | 8,000 | 55,000 | n.a. | 22,000 | 10,300 |
| Military expenditure (in $ millions) | n.a. | 659 | 15,512 | 64 | 4,055 | 1,392 |
| Military expenditure (as a % of GDP) | n.a. | 1.3 | 2.7 | 0.8 | 5.3 | 5.9 |

Table 3.1 (continued)

| | 2005 | | | | | |
|---|---|---|---|---|---|---|
| | *Afghanistan* | *Bangladesh* | *India* | *Nepal* | *Pakistan* | *Sri Lanka* |
| Total Armed Forces | 27,000 | 125,500 | 1,325,000 | 69,000 | 619,000 | 111,000 |
| Army | 27,000 | 110,000 | 1,100,000 | 69,000 | 550,000 | 78,100 |
| Air Force | n.a. | 6,500 | 170,000 | n.a. | 45,000 | 18,000 |
| Navy | n.a. | 9,000 | 55,000 | n.a. | 24,000 | 15,000 |
| Military expenditure (in $ millions) | 163 | 795 | 28,295 | 206 | 5,210 | 934 |
| Military expenditure (as a % of GDP) | 1.7 | 1 | 2.8 | 2.2 | 3.4 | 2.6 |

Source: IISS, The Military Balance, for data on conventional armed forces. SIPRI Yearbook, for data on military expenditures.
* data on 1985 military expenditures rely on 1988 figures.

The existing conventional force capabilities of SAARC member states suggest that India is the dominant regional player. Moreover, as I will argue elsewhere in this book, India's supremacy in the region will escalate because Pakistan will be unable to sustain a long-term conventional arms race with India, largely as a result of its heavy debt burden and the consequent fiscal pressures that this imposes on the country.[29]

Given the inherent asymmetry in military capabilities, SAARC has attempted to sidestep any resulting controversy by addressing other security-related concerns of mutual interest. Since the association's inception, the largest share of SAARC conventions and agreements has dealt with various aspects of security, broadly defined. As Table 3.2 shows, a number of conventions, an additional protocol on security, and some agreements on food security have been signed. In practice, though, some observers have expressed doubt about the impact of these agreements. Kishore Dash has noted, for instance, that "the much talked about SAARC Food Security Reserve could not be utilized to meet the needs of Bangladesh during its worst natural disaster in 1991. The Convention on Suppression of Terrorism appears to be a failure, as both India and Pakistan have failed to curtail the movements of terrorists across their borders."[30] A SAARC-sponsored committee report goes further in its criticism. According to the report of the SAARC group of eminent persons, "the facilities provided under the SAARC Food Security

*Table 3.2* SAARC conventions, protocols, and agreements on security, 1985–2010

| *Conventions and protocols on security* | *Date of signing* |
|---|---|
| SAARC regional convention on suppression of terrorism | 4 November 1987 |
| SAARC convention on narcotics, drugs, and psychotropic substances | 23 November 1990 |
| SAARC convention on regional arrangements for the promotion of child welfare in South Asia | 5 January 2002 |
| SAARC convention on preventing and combating trafficking in women and children for prostitution | 5 January 2002 |
| Additional protocol to the SAARC regional convention on suppression of terrorism | 6 January 2004 |
| *Agreements on security* | |
| Agreement on establishing the SAARC food security reserve | 4 November 1987 |
| Agreement on establishing the SAARC security food bank | 3 April 2007 |

Source: SAARC Secretariat.

Reserve have never been utilized even though member countries have suffered from acute food shortage from time to time. The Conventions on Suppression of Terrorism have had no impact on controlling terrorism or drug trafficking through regional cooperation in South Asia."[31]

A cursory examination of Table 3.2 shows that the prevention of terrorism has been formally viewed as an important topic by SAARC members. However, the concept of terrorism is an inherently politicized subject because there is no general consensus on who is a terrorist and what constitutes a terrorist act. Within the context of South Asia in particular, there have been wide discrepancies on whether armed insurgency movements in the Pakistani state of Baluchistan, the Indian states of Punjab and Jammu and Kashmir, Nepal, or Sri Lanka, represent movements of national self-determination or terrorism. Central governments in South Asia have tended to label such instances of internal armed insurgencies as constituting terrorism.

Given the controversial nature of terrorism, it should be surprising to observe that the 1987 SAARC Convention on Suppression of Terrorism was the first regional convention on security matters. The 1987 SAARC convention attempts to define terrorist acts in accordance with those offered in other international accords, namely the 1970 Convention for the Suppression of Unlawful Seizure of Aircraft, the 1971 Convention for the Suppression of Unlawful Acts against the Safety of Civil Aviation, and the 1973 Convention on the Prevention and Punishment of Crimes against Internationally Protected Persons, including Diplomatic Agents. The 1987 SAARC Convention on Suppression of Terrorism also provides for a protocol on the initiation of extradition proceedings. In this respect, the 1987 convention is emphatic regarding the issue of the obligations of contracting states. For instance, Article 6 of the 1987 convention provides that a contracting state "in whose territory an alleged offender is found, shall, upon receiving a request for extradition from another Contracting State, take appropriate measures, subject to its national laws, so as to ensure his presence for purposes of extradition or prosecution."[32] However, given the 1987 convention's reliance on the definition of terrorism based on the hijacking of airplanes and actions against internationally protected persons, it would appear that a more comprehensive and contemporary understanding of terrorism is not envisioned.

Over the years, India has maintained that Pakistan has harbored and offered support to a number of Kashmiri and Punjabi separatist militant groups. In some instances, these groups have launched noteworthy armed attacks on the Jammu and Kashmir legislative assembly (1 October 2001) and India's national parliament (13 December 2001). Other prominent terrorist attacks in New Delhi and Mumbai have also been viewed as acts resulting from infiltration by terrorists across the India-Pakistan border. In order to remedy that situation, the Indian government has taken steps to curtail the transit of terrorists and armament across the India-Pakistan border by building a fence along the actual line of control separating both countries. In its 2009–10 annual report, India's Ministry of Home Affairs has declared that the India-Pakistan border is "characterized by attempts at infiltration by terrorists and smuggling of arms, ammunition and contraband."[33] Pakistan has vehemently denied involvement in supporting cross-border attacks by terrorist groups. Nevertheless, independent analysts on cross-border terrorism differ on that assessment. For instance, an analyst of cross-border terrorist activities in India has argued, quite unequivocally, that "India has remained a victim of cross-border terrorism since gaining its independence from the British. Pakistan's propensity for using non-state actors as proxies to fight its wars goes back to 1947 and the founding of the Pakistani state, and has continued to the present."[34] Another prominent analyst of security in South Asia has also asserted that Pakistan has "long been a sponsor of terrorism" and has "faced considerable blow-back from several of these terrorist groups, most importantly from elements of the Taliban."[35]

Since the signing of the 1987 SAARC Convention on Suppression of Terrorism, there has been little movement towards a coordinated, SAARC-led effort to suppress and prevent terrorism. In 1995, eight years after the 1987 convention was signed, the most tangible outcome of multilateral cooperation on terrorism was the establishment of a SAARC Terrorist Offenses Monitoring Desk (STOMD), based in Colombo, Sri Lanka. The stated purpose of the STOMD is to collate, analyze, and disseminate information about terrorist incidents, tactics, funding mechanisms, and strategies. However, it would be erroneous to think that the STOMD has been, or is likely to be, a major force in the fight against terrorism. For instance, in an assessment of counterterrorism measures, the chair of the meeting of legal advisors of SAARC member states, briefed the SAARC Standing Committee on the "constraints faced by the STOMD due to lack of [a] regular flow of information from member states." He also highlighted "the lack of communication between the focal points on a regular basis, as the major constraint faced in the functioning of the Desk."[36]

Individual member states have attempted to strengthen their ability to combat and suppress terrorism by enacting domestic legislation that mirrors the 1987 convention. For instance, in 1988, the Sri Lankan parliament adopted the SAARC Regional Convention on Suppression of Terrorism Act no. 70 in order to provide enabling domestic legislation in accordance with the 1987 convention. Similarly, in 1993, the Indian parliament enacted the 1993 SAARC Convention (Suppression of Terrorism) Act for the purpose of providing comprehensive effect to all the provisions of the 1987 SAARC Convention on Suppression of Terrorism.[37] Acknowledging that India does not possess extradition treaties with all SAARC member states, the 1993 Act recognizes the 1987 SAARC convention as the legal basis for extradition with states with which India does not have an extradition treaty. Operating under international legal provisions, India has attempted to exercise the option of initiating extradition procedures in a number of cases. However, its success at securing extradition through this mechanism has been very limited.[38]

The reason for the weakness in the extradition clauses of the 1987 convention is that Article 7 of the said convention also provides that contracting states shall not be obliged to extradite "if it appears to the requested State that by reason of the trivial nature of the case or by reason of the request for the surrender or return of a fugitive offender not being made in good faith or in the interests of justice or for any other reason it is unjust or inexpedient to surrender or return the fugitive offender."[39]

In order to close other loopholes in the 1987 SAARC Convention on Suppression of Terrorism, at the 11th SAARC summit held in January 2002 in Colombo, SAARC member states agreed to reiterate their determination to prevent and suppress terrorism and reaffirmed their commitment to fully implement the 1987 convention. This led to the signing of an additional protocol to the 1987 convention at the 12th SAARC summit held in January 2004 in Islamabad, Pakistan. Following individual ratification by SAARC member states, the additional protocol has provided greater detail on the measures to prevent, suppress and eradicate the financing of terrorist activities. Article 7 of the 2004 additional protocol calls for the adoption of a "comprehensive domestic and supervisory regime for banks, other financial institutions and other entities deemed particularly susceptible to being used for the financing of terrorist activities."[40] However, little has been done to actually implement the recommendations of the 2004 additional protocol.

Given the stated commitment by SAARC member states to suppress terrorism, one may be tempted to conclude that the association's record on security matters is a positive one. However, independent analysis questions the usefulness of SAARC as an institutional mechanism to suppress terrorism. One observer concluded that "SAARC has not made any serious effort to implement the provisions of the convention. At the 15th SAARC summit held in Colombo in 2008, leaders again took a pledge to fight terrorism collectively, but in reality SAARC has not made any progress forward on this matter."[41] Sumit Ganguly also offers a pessimistic assessment of the ability of SAARC to act as an institutional mechanism to cooperate effectively in regional counterterrorism measures. In his view, "SAARC is institutionally hamstrung from undertaking the task of multilateral counterterrorism cooperation. The association's charter formally prohibits the discussion of 'bilateral and contentious' issues, and so tackling the vexed question of regional counterterrorism cooperation is not entirely within its purview."[42]

## Economic cooperation

In showing how political conditions shape regionalism, Edward Mansfield and Helen Milner argue that much of the research on the dynamics of regional cooperation focuses on international trade. They contend that within this framework one important strand of literature suggests that "whether states choose to enter regional trade arrangements and the economic effects of these arrangements depend on the preferences of national policymakers and interest groups, as well as the nature and strength of domestic institutions."[43] On the basis of South Asia's experience with intraregional trade, one may conclude that the preferences of national policymakers and interest groups in South Asia are not to trade with other South Asian countries.

South Asia appears to be an exception to the theoretical expectation that the dynamics of regional cooperation are linked to levels of international trade. A cursory examination of the degree of intraregional trade points to little engagement among SAARC members. For instance, Table 3.3 shows that, with the exception of Nepal, most South Asian nations traded little with other SAARC members at the time of SAARC's foundation in 1985. Since then, trade between individual South Asian countries and other SAARC members has grown very gradually over time, with some declines in 1995. The gradual increase in trade patterns appears to hold for 2005. As Table 3.3 shows, only the Maldives and Sri Lanka have increased their trade with other South Asian nations steadily over time.

Table 3.3 illustrates the percentage of imports and exports from a given South Asian country to the rest of South Asia. The trade patterns for individual countries show that India and Pakistan trade little with the rest of South Asia relative to trade worldwide. For instance, imports from the rest of South Asia to India (the largest economy in the region) amounted to less than one percent of India's overall imports

*Table 3.3* Percentage of trade between individual South Asian countries with the rest of South Asia

| *Year/country* | *1985* | | *1995* | | *2005* | |
|---|---|---|---|---|---|---|
| | *Imports* | *Exports* | *Imports* | *Exports* | *Imports* | *Exports* |
| Afghanistan | 8.5 | 17.0 | 10.3 | 12.6 | 44.8 | 41.1 |
| Bangladesh | 3.5 | 7.8 | 17.7 | 2.7 | 15.2 | 2.2 |
| India | 0.8 | 3.4 | 0.6 | 5.1 | 0.9 | 5.4 |
| Maldives | 10.0 | 19.9 | 13.2 | 22.6 | 17.4 | 17.4 |
| Nepal | 32.4 | 38.3 | 17.2 | 9.2 | 59.7 | 67.4 |
| Pakistan | 1.9 | 5.8 | 1.6 | 3.4 | 3.0 | 11.2 |
| Sri Lanka | 6.4 | 4.6 | 12.2 | 2.7 | 22.4 | 10.3 |

Source: IMF, *Direction of Trade Statistics*. Figures represent the percentage of trade by a single country with the rest of South Asia as a proportion of trade worldwide. Data calculated by the author using reporting country data.

worldwide. Likewise, Pakistan (South Asia's second largest trader) imported little from other South Asian countries as a proportion of that country's overall imports worldwide.

Table 3.3 also shows that only the trading patterns of one or two South Asian countries with their neighbors are substantial. For instance, over 59 percent of Nepal's imports in 2005 came from other South Asian countries and over 67 percent of its exports in 2005 went to other South Asian countries. Among the selected countries, Afghanistan also shows strong trade links with other South Asian countries (particularly in 2005). In 2005, over 44 percent of Afghanistan's imports came from South Asia and over 40 percent of its exports went to South Asia. Nevertheless, one should be careful about interpreting the significance of these trade patterns. The actual trade volume from these two landlocked countries is actually quite small. Nepal's global imports in 2005 amounted to a little over US $2 billion, Afghanistan's global imports during the same year amounted to US $2.9 billion.[44] Moreover, most of the trade between Nepal and Afghanistan with the rest of South Asia is limited to one country. For instance, over 59 percent of Nepal's global imports in 2005 came from India, while 39 percent of Afghanistan's global imports in 2005 came from Pakistan. In other words, countries like Nepal and Afghanistan do not have diversified destinations for imports or exports with the rest of South Asia; they merely restrict their limited trade volume to one country.

In addition to the challenges suggested by Mansfield and Milner, inherent structural impediments offer an explanation for the pattern of South Asia's trade dynamics. As I argue elsewhere in this book, South Asian countries trade little with each other because they are not trade congruent, and principally because there is little demand for one another's exports.[45] For most countries in South Asia—particularly Bangladesh, Pakistan, and Sri Lanka—the leading commodity for export is textiles. These economies do not have a highly diversified export platform. Moreover, the ongoing political and military rivalry between South Asia's two largest economies (India and Pakistan) inhibits trade relations for most commodities.

In light of the inherent structural economic and trade challenges, one of the stated objectives of SAARC, as articulated in its Charter, has been to foster the acceleration of economic growth and the promotion of active collaboration in economic issues. Following the first SAARC summit, the first ministerial meeting on international economic issues was held in Islamabad from 31 March to 3 April 1986. The declaration that emerged from this meeting supported the proposal for stronger regional cooperation on trade and economic matters, but also agreed that there should be greater institutional coordination between the national planning offices of the SAARC member states.

A series of analytical studies undertaken at the behest of the national planning offices of SAARC member states helped to identify priority areas for South Asian regional cooperation on trade, manufacturing, and services. Subsequently, the view prevailed that a higher level of institutionalization was needed to carry out the recommendations stemming from the analytical studies on South Asian trade and economic cooperation. To that effect, during the ninth session of the Council of Ministers' meeting in Malé, Maldives, it was proposed that a high level committee on economic cooperation should be established. This was called the Committee on Economic Cooperation (CEC).

The membership of the CEC was composed of the commerce and trade secretaries from all the SAARC member states. From an institutional perspective, the CEC helped to promote intraregional trade, largely by formulating initiatives relating to preferential trading arrangements and trade harmonization between SAARC member states. More importantly, the CEC also endorsed the idea that South Asia's limited trade presence worldwide was a result of the largely autarkic trade regimes that had prevailed in South Asia since the 1960s. To counteract overly protectionist trade policies, one of the key proposals advanced by the CEC was the recommendation that an Intergovernmental Group (IGG) be created to formulate and seek agreement on an institutional framework under which specific trade liberalization measures could be enacted. According to Syed, "over the years, the CEC has emerged as one of the most important groups within the SAARC having a mandate over economic and trade issues."[46]

The growing necessity for greater intraregional trade took place in the midst of severe economic dislocations in South Asia. The Iraqi invasion of Kuwait in August 1990 and the international embargo that followed had very direct negative effects on all South Asian economies. The combination of a substantial decline in remittances with a sharp increase in the price of crude oil and natural gas imports imperiled the current and capital accounts from South Asia. In June 1991, India suffered a major balance of payments crisis. Not surprisingly, the issue of economic interdependence was the key theme at the SAARC summit held in Colombo on 21 December 1991. At the conclusion of the summit, the declaration emphasized "the need for vigorously promoting South-South economic cooperation to offset the negative consequences of international economic developments."[47]

Based on the recommendation of the CEC, SAARC accepted the proposal to create an IGG. In a more assertive move, though, the 1991 SAARC summit declaration also encouraged the examination of a Sri Lankan proposal for the establishment of a SAARC Preferential Trade Arrangement (SAPTA) by 1997. Sri Lanka, an economy that is heavily reliant on exports, had taken aggressive initiatives to diversify trade and enhance intraregional trade based on the economic policies of Sri Lankan prime ministers Dingiri Banda Wijetunga (1989–93) and, especially, Ranil Wickramasinghe (1993–4). Wickamansinghe had been responsible for the expansion of the Biyagama export processing zone (EPZ) and the implementation of the Koggala EPZ in the early 1990s, economic initiatives that were highly controversial at the time.[48]

The collective efforts for the creation of a multilateral trading arrangement in South Asia culminated in the signing of SAPTA. The agreement was signed on 11 April 1993, at the conclusion of the seventh SAARC summit held in Dhaka, Bangladesh. The key components of SAPTA concerned arrangements on tariffs, non-tariff barriers and paratariffs, non-tariff measures and direct tariff measures. SAPTA provided a range of modalities under which negotiations for greater trade liberalization could take place. One of the key characteristics of SAPTA concerned specific provisions and safeguards for the least developed contracting states. Article 10 of the agreement specified areas where the least developed contracting states would enjoy special and favorable treatment.

It is important to note that the drive for greater economic cooperation within South Asia was also built on the support and encouragement from the domestic private sector. Within the scope of SAARC-related institutions, the SAARC Chambers of Commerce and Industry (SCCI) was established in 1992. The SCCI encouraged the facilitation of trade relations between South Asian countries. In the estimation of

M. H. Syed, the SCCI "was instrumental in bringing into fruition the SAARC Preferential Trading Arrangement (SAPTA)."[49]

Although the 1991 SAARC summit declaration had called for the establishment of a SAPTA by 1997, the high level of consensus among South Asian leaders was such that the actual date of establishment of this trade mechanism was moved forward by two years. With the creation of a SAPTA in December 1995, several rounds of trade liberalization negotiations took place. The first two rounds of SAPTA trade negotiations were structured around a single negotiation modality, namely on a product-by-product basis. Eventually, during the third round of SAPTA negotiations, a chapter-wise negotiating modality was introduced. The fourth round of SAPTA negotiations was open to a wider range of modalities, including across-the-board tariff reduction, sectoral tariff reduction, and direct trade measures.

While supporting the concept of SAPTA, some critics began to bemoan the slow pace of trade concessions on commodities. According to Indra Nath Mukherji, an advocate of greater current account liberalization in the region, "the product-by-product approach to trade negotiations was inherently protracted and time-consuming."[50] Other criticisms of SAPTA have noted that trade concessions were not shared equitably among South Asian states. For instance, noting the perceived asymmetrical level of concessions, Mukherji argued that "except for India, none of the other contracting states has conceded meaningful tariff cuts. The effects of trade liberalisation are thus modest."[51] A third stream of criticism centered on the idea that given the inherent asymmetries in the economic strength of South Asian countries, greater focus should be placed on the protection of smaller trade partners.

Frustration about the slow pace of trade liberalization under SAPTA prompted South Asian leaders to stress the need to accelerate the progress of SAPTA negotiations. Moreover, SAARC began to provide a more direct link between trade liberalization measures and the establishment of a South Asia free trade area, provided that the special circumstances of smaller member states were accommodated. In the declaration issued at the conclusion of the 1997 SAARC summit in Malé, the delegates "recognized the importance of achieving a free trade area by the year 2001 AD and reiterated that steps towards trade liberalisation must take into account the special needs of the smaller and the Least Developed Countries and that benefits must accrue equitably."[52]

Despite some evidence of improvements in the breadth and scope of SAPTA trade liberalization negotiations, there was a growing impatience with the existing outcomes. For instance, in the declaration issued at the conclusion of the 1998 summit in Colombo, SAARC leaders put forth a more precise and sharply worded admonition "that to accelerate progress in the next round of SAPTA negotiations, deeper preferential tariff concessions should be extended to products which are being actively traded, or are likely to be traded, among Members; that discriminatory practices and non-tariff barriers should be simultaneously removed on items in respect of which tariff concessions are granted or have been granted earlier."[53]

In order to address the issue of multilateral compliance, at the 1998 SAARC summit, South Asian leaders also began to propose a more precise timetable for the implementation of tariff reductions. Similarly, the orientation of SAARC agreements began to shift more concretely towards the establishment of a South Asia free trade area (or SAFTA). The SCCI had delineated a plan entitled "Road Map to SAFTA," geared at facilitating the engagement of the private sector in the governmental efforts to enhance regional integration. Responding to these demands, South Asian leaders decided that a Committee of Experts, in consultation with SAARC member states, be constituted and entrusted with precise terms of reference for the purpose of defining the characteristics of a SAFTA. The 1998 summit declaration acknowledged the SCCI's contribution and welcomed its proposal to engage South Asia's private sector in SAARC export promotion activities.

However, the remit of the newly constituted Committee of Experts overlapped with an existing Inter-Governmental Expert Group (IGEG) that had been created after a proposal made at the 16th session of the Council of Ministers held in New Delhi, India, on 18–19 September 1995. The objective of the IGEG had been to identify the necessary steps that would be needed to achieve a free trade area in South Asia. In contrast to this, the Committee of Experts set out to draft a comprehensive multilateral treaty that would outline the institutional and regulatory framework of SAFTA.

As SAARC began to consider the creation of a South Asia free trade area, it became evident that there were a range of parallel structural obstacles—beyond those specific to trade—that inhibited greater intraregional economic cooperation. Various SAARC summit declarations had pointed to a range of such impediments, including developing adequate transportation infrastructure and communication links among SAARC member states. In order to increase complementarities in economic activities, SAARC also welcomed the initiation of specific steps to promote and protect investment.

The Agreement on South Asian Free Trade Area (SAFTA) was eventually signed on 6 January 2004 at the conclusion of the 12th SAARC summit held in Islamabad. The agreement became operational in July

2006, following ratification by all SAARC member states. The Agreement on SAFTA is undeniably the most important intraregional trade agreement in South Asia and is, arguably, the most significant achievement of SAARC. The agreement provided for the adoption of various instruments of trade liberalization on a preferential basis. According to Article 4 of the agreement, the SAFTA agreement would be implemented through the adoption of a trade liberalization program, a coordinated agreement on rules of origin, safeguard measures, and the establishment of institutional arrangements, consultations and dispute settlement procedures.[54] This call for greater liberalization should be weighed in relation to the fact that unlike the mechanism provided by SAARC, South Asian countries are engaged in over 20 multilateral and 20 bilateral trade agreements.

On the basis of these implementation instruments, SAARC has, since its inception, adopted six agreements facilitating trade-related and investment service provision across South Asia. As Table 3.4 shows, the Agreement on SAFTA has, however, jumpstarted several agreements on trade facilitation measures, including agreements on mutual administrative assistance on customs matters and an agreement on the prevention of double taxation. Aside from these procedural agreements, SAARC has also facilitated the creation of two institutions that are auxiliary to trade: the SAARC Arbitration Council and the SAARC Regional Standards Organization (SARSO).

The 2005 agreement on the establishment of a SAARC Arbitration Council is important because it recognizes the need to provide a coherent legal framework within South Asia for the settlement of commercial

*Table 3.4* SAARC agreements on trade and service provision

| *Agreements on trade* | *Date of signing* |
|---|---|
| Agreement on SAARC Preferential Trading Arrangement (SAPTA) | 11 April 1993 |
| Agreement on South Asian Free Trade Area (SAFTA) | 6 January 2004 |
| Agreement on Mutual Administrative Assistance on Customs Matters | 13 November 2005 |
| SAARC Multilateral Agreement on Avoidance of Double Taxation and Mutual Administrative Assistance in Tax Matters | 13 November 2005 |
| Agreement for Establishment of SAARC Arbitration Council | 13 November 2005 |
| Agreement on the Establishment of South Asian Regional Standards Organization (SARSO) | 3 August 2008 |

Source: SAARC Secretariat.

disputes.[55] This development is particularly necessary in the context of legal systems that are not renowned for being expeditious. The SAARC Arbitration Council seeks to promote the growth of national arbitration institutions and to act as a coordinating agency in a regional dispute settlement system. However, the SAARC Arbitration Council is still in an infant stage of development, having received the nomination for its first director general and the approval for the establishment of a secretariat in Islamabad in 2010.

The 2005 agreement on mutual administrative assistance on customs matters and the SAARC multilateral agreement on the avoidance of double taxation and mutual administrative assistance in tax matters demonstrates that there is some nominal consensus that South Asian countries should minimize transaction costs in trade and investment-related matters. On the agreement on the avoidance of double taxation, SAARC member states appear to have begun to support a minimum threshold in the sharing of tax-related information between the competent authorities of the relevant states. They also agree, in principle, to lending assistance to other SAARC member states in the collection of revenue claims.[56] Finally, the 2005 agreement also provides broad guidelines on the avoidance of double taxation by key population subgroups (e.g., professors, researchers, students). Similarly, in the SAARC agreement on mutual administrative assistance on customs matters, SAARC member states pledged to provide the customs administrations of other SAARC member states with information and intelligence relating to the prevention, investigation, and prosecution of customs-related offenses.[57]

Likewise, the 2008 agreement on the establishment of the SARSO also shows that the association's ancillary institutions could provide useful outcomes for its member states. The principal aim of SARSO is to "develop harmonised standards for the region to facilitate intra-regional trade and to have access in the global market."[58] These objectives correspond with the guidelines advocated by the International Organization for Standardization (ISO) and other similar international standards organizations, like the International Electrotechnical Commission (IEC).[59] The 2008 agreement on the establishment of SARSO outlines a detailed institutional structure for the organization. SARSO is to be based in Dhaka and it is expected that over the next few years it will have a director general, a secretariat (assisted by a technical management team), and a governing body.[60]

Although less numerous than those relating to security, it could be argued that SAARC agreements on trade are having more impact in the short term. These incipient institutions are beginning to provide tangible evidence of an institutional framework of regional cooperation.

Nevertheless, it may be premature to suggest that the 2004 SAFTA has dramatically increased trade among SAARC members. Figures 3.1 and 3.2 show the increase of trade among all SAARC members.[61] With some exceptions, the level of imports and exports by individual countries to and from the other SAARC member states has increased substantially since 2004.

Figure 3.1 shows that, since the signing of the 2004 SAFTA, the levels of imports from other SAARC member states to Afghanistan and Pakistan have increased dramatically, with nearly a threefold percentage increase for both countries. Meanwhile, India's imports from other SAARC member states have increased twofold.

Similarly to the increase in the level of imports from other SAARC member countries, Figure 3.2 shows that, since the signing of the 2004 SAFTA, the percentage increase of exports from individual SAARC member states to other association members has risen rapidly. As Figure 3.2 shows, the rate of increase is particularly impressive in the case of Bangladesh, whose exports to other SAARC members have risen threefold. On the other hand, it is worth stressing that the percentage increase of trade between Nepal and the Maldives and other SAARC member states has been more modest, and in the case of Sri

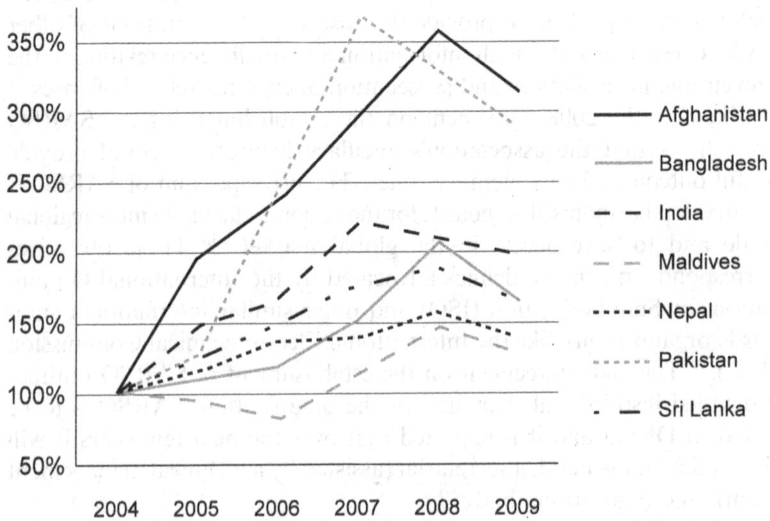


*Figure 3.1* Percentage increase in the level of imports of individual SAARC member states with other SAARC members (2004 = 100), 2004–9
Source: IMF, *Direction of Trade Statistics*

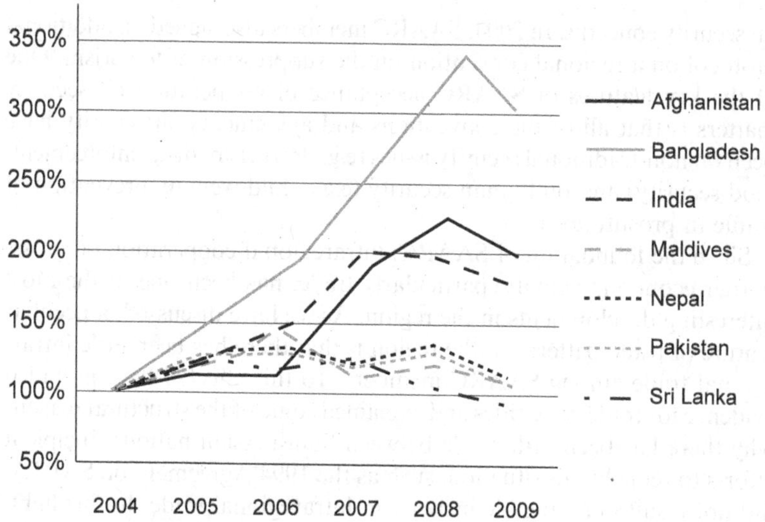


*Figure 3.2* Percentage increase in the level of exports of individual SAARC member states with other SAARC members (2004 = 100), 2004–9

Source: IMF, *Direction of Trade Statistics*

Lanka, it has declined relative to the percentage levels of Sri Lanka's intraregional trade with other SAARC members.

## Conclusion

We have evaluated the trends in SAARC intraregional collaboration on the issues of security and trade. This analysis has been framed within the context of the literature in international relations theory on the effectiveness of international organizations. As was suggested at the start of this chapter, neorealist and structural interdependence perspectives differ in the assessment of what precisely constitutes international organization effectiveness. A running theme in the discussion of the effectiveness of SAARC has been the inherent asymmetry between its member states, particularly in the areas of military and economic capabilities.

Furthermore, we have examined the institution's intention to enhance intraregional collaboration in security matters. Predictably, SAARC cooperation in this area has been circumscribed by more general geopolitical concerns about the region. In this chapter, though, I have shown that there has been a demonstrable commitment to intraregional collaboration on security, broadly defined. For instance, the association's member states have signed a significant number of conventions on security concerns. In 2004, SAARC members also signed an additional protocol on a regional convention on the suppression of terrorism. One of the key features of SAARC acceptance of cooperation on security matters is that all of the conventions and agreements on security have been on non-traditional security issues (e.g., terrorism, drug enforcement, food security) and on human security (e.g., child welfare, prevention of traffic in prostitution).

Since the foundation of SAARC, intraregional cooperation on cross-border economic activity, particularly trade, has been one of the most interesting developments in the region. As we have discussed, a peculiar feature of trade patterns in the region is that there has been little intraregional trade among SAARC members. To this effect, I have provided evidence for trade disparities and explained some of the structural reasons why there has been little trade between South Asian nations. Incipient efforts to remedy this situation, such as the 1994 Agreement on SAPTA, did not result in a tangible increase in intraregional trade. In this light, SAARC commitment to increase economic interdependence in the region has proven to be a test case of the effectiveness of this regional organization. As argued here, the 2004 SAFTA will probably be seen as one of the most important developments in the region to be initiated by SAARC. Moreover, I have shown that the annual percentage growth in intraregional trade has been substantial since 2004, particularly for Afghanistan and Pakistan in terms of imports and Bangladesh and Pakistan in terms of exports to other SAARC member states.

The findings from this chapter should be tempered against the expectation that SAARC has been either a success or a failure. The nominal cooperation on security matters reached at SAARC has not involved traditional security issues, such as conventional force deployment. Inevitably, India and Pakistan's traditional enmity transforms discussions about security into a bilateral issue, hence outside the stated remit of this regional body. Curiously, the association's aversion to the discussion of controversial issues has not inhibited developments in economic cooperation and trade. Nevertheless, it should be noted that, despite the increase in intraregional trade following the signing of the 2004 SAFTA, intraregional trade as a proportion of a SAARC member country's trade worldwide has not changed noticeably. Similarly, the apparent increase in intraregional trade evidenced since 2004 has been due to increasing volumes of trade between particular partners, for example, Afghani imports from Pakistan, and Bangladeshi exports to India.

# 4 The dimensions of regional collaboration in South Asia

- Regional integration and SAARC
- The integrated program of action
- Collaboration on human capital and social infrastructure
- SAARC regional centers, apex and recognized bodies
- Conclusion

Despite some developmental improvements in recent decades, South Asia remains one of the poorest regions in the world, comparable in many respects to sub-Saharan Africa. For instance, according to the World Bank, the poverty headcount ratio at US $1.25 a day was 40 percent in South Asia and 53 percent in sub-Saharan Africa.[1] Given their limited fiscal resources, individual countries in South Asia are often ill-equipped to single-handedly tackle most of their internal developmental problems. Thus, there is a strong incentive to seek external support to alleviate domestic developmental challenges. For instance, South Asian countries have been world-leading recipients of net overseas development assistance from the International Development Association's (IDA) assistance fund for the world's poorest countries.[2] As an alternative funding mechanism, SAARC has endeavored to enhance regional collaboration on human capital and social infrastructure, principally through a mixture of top-down and bottom-up programs.

From the outset it should be useful to frame the dimensions of SAARC's regional collaboration efforts within the context of the literature on comparative regional integration. The theoretical literature will guide us to understand how regional integration can take place, particularly in situations where there is a considerable level of asymmetry in state capacity to tackle developmental problems. In this chapter I will highlight the efforts that SAARC has made in defining its remit through the creation of an integrated program of action (IPA). I will show that the association's efforts to list subject areas for inclusion in the IPA have resulted in a diffuse range of overlapping objectives, with no clear indication that SAARC has been successful at implementing any single individual subject area contained in the IPA. In this chapter I will also examine the development of SAARC's elaborate institutional framework to facilitate regional collaboration, particularly with the establishment of SAARC regional centers, apex and recognized bodies. The SAARC regional centers and other ancillary institutional bodies are expected to provide a bottom-up approach to regional collaboration. I will conclude by determining whether any of these institutions have helped to deepen regional integration in South Asia.

## Regional integration and SAARC

The neofunctionalist literature on comparative regional integration highlights the importance of building a commonality of interest in light of increased economic and political complementarities. Within the context of emerging regional integration in Europe, Ernst Haas defined integration as "the process whereby political actors in several distinct national settings are persuaded to shift their loyalties, expectations and political activities toward a new center, whose institutions possess or demand jurisdiction over the pre-existing national states."[3]

The literature on regional integration in Asia has also stressed the need for an emerging political community, though the threshold for the development of such a web of economic, social, and political interdependence may be higher due to the expectation of consensus or (in the case of SAARC) unanimity in the adoption of supranational decisions.

Subsequent pioneering efforts by Joseph Nye and other neoliberal institutionalists to operationalize the levels of regional integration suggest that this can be of three types: economic (leading to the formation of a transnational economy in trade and services); social (mass and elite level interactions, contributing to the formation of a transnational society); and political (institutional, policy, attitudinal, and security community engagement, leading to the formation of transnational political interdependence).[4] In the previous chapter I discussed two critical areas of regional cooperation (i.e., military and strategic cooperation, and trade). Given SAARC's decision-making mechanism on the basis of unanimity, it is curious to note that during the initial stages of forming the association, at least one member state raised objections regarding the proposed collaboration on trade and education, two areas where greater regional cooperation has been achieved.

The case of regional integration among SAARC countries is interesting because the level of asymmetry between the member states is high, yet the association operates on the expectation of unanimity. The tensions caused by this institutional asymmetry have been compounded by the acrimonious bilateral relationship between the association's two largest members, namely India and Pakistan. As he departed to attend the first SAARC summit, India's prime minister Rajiv Gandhi attempted to allay fears that India's presence would dominate the proceedings and observed that "ours is going to be a meeting of equal and sovereign partners in the common quest for a better future for our peoples."[5] However, the internal sensitivities about the potentially dominant role that India could play in the association were raised explicitly by Pakistan's president Zia-ul-Haq on the eve of the first SAARC summit. In an interview in the *Bangladesh Observer*, one of Bangladesh's principal dailies, the theme of India's potential central role in the association and the recognition that there is an inherent asymmetry among SAARC members were core points in President Zia's remarks. For instance, President Zia argued that "through SARC we hope to convince India that it must take measures to play its part as the center figure in South Asia but with a recognition that there is nobody big or small."[6] President Zia added that India "with whom we would like to join hands and be in the mainstream and play much more of a role which can generate confidence rather than fear for smaller neighbours."[7]

President Zia's comments in the *Bangladesh Observer* generated a great deal of controversy in the Indian press, namely because they sidestepped his call to "join hands" and his recognition of India's central role in South Asia. Instead, the Indian press seized on the purported fear of India by the region's smaller countries. For instance, one of India's most respected newspapers, the *Hindustan Times,* quoted President Zia as having remarked in the *Bangladesh Observer* that "India must play a positive role to allay the fears of the small neighbours and instill trust and confidence in them."[8] Although one may disagree with President Zia's remarks about India's role in SAARC, he never actually used the words that were attributed to him in the *Hindustan Times.* Nevertheless, India's prime minister, Rajiv Gandhi, was pressured to respond to President Zia's alleged provocation. Gandhi vehemently denied that SAARC would be tilted in favor of India. Rejecting President Zia's comments, Gandhi emphasized that "everyone in SAARC is equal."[9]

The notion of asymmetry among SAARC members, though, has been at the center of the conceptualization of the association. For instance, in outlining the expected contribution of SAARC to regional cooperation, Bangladesh's foreign secretary Faruq Choudhury argued that the "strength of the SARC lies in the spontaneous and autonomous character of the association of the states in the region and their unanimity on the integrated action programme."[10] In reacting to the criticism that SAARC has an asymmetric composition, Choudhury agreed that asymmetry "can admittedly be a source of predicament for weaker neighbours" but argued that "disparity in military and economic strength is not peculiar to the South Asian region. It is in fact a global phenomenon and found to exist in varying degrees in all regions and sub-regions."[11]

In Chapter 3 I noted important achievements relating to security and trade. Cooperation appears to have been particularly promising in areas where the possibility of contentious issues arising is highest. This chapter will illustrate SAARC's hesitant efforts to promote regional collaboration through its regional centers. Curiously, there has been little collaboration on issues not dealing with security or trade. Since the association's inception, there have only been two SAARC agreements: one on the establishment of a SAARC arbitration council and the other on the establishment of a South Asian university.

In attempting to build unanimity on issues not pertaining directly to military security and economic cooperation, South Asia has pursued a state-promoted, "bottom-up" approach to regional cooperation, principally at the instigation of smaller and weaker individual states. According to one early analysis of the prospects of regional cooperation, smaller countries "because of their fear of domination by India, have carefully evolved for themselves separate identities through international contacts and agreements."[12] On this basis it could be inferred that the growth of regionalism in South Asia, mediated through regional institutions like SAARC, is an effort to restrict the free exercise of hegemonic power by India. In November 1980, the government of Bangladesh circulated a working paper which outlined 11 proposed areas of cooperation in the fields of telecommunications, transport, shipping, tourism, agriculture and rural sector development, joint venture and market promotion in selected commodities, science and technological collaboration, education, and culture.[13]

The government of Bangladesh's draft paper provided the basis for the discussions that took place at the inaugural foreign secretaries' meeting held in Colombo, Sri Lanka, on 21–23 April 1981. At the conclusion of the meeting, the delegates issued a joint communiqué identifying five critical areas for regional cooperation: agriculture, rural development, telecommunications, meteorology, and health and population activities.[14] In order to carry out in-depth analyses of these areas, the foreign secretaries also agreed to set up five study groups, each entrusted with the task of making concrete recommendations at a later date. Bangladesh was expected to sponsor studies relating to agriculture, Sri Lanka would tackle rural development, Pakistan would handle telecommunications, India would specialize in meteorology, and Nepal would address issues relating to health and population activities.

The 1981 foreign secretaries' meeting in Colombo was significant because it framed future institutional arrangements for regional cooperation.[15] According to one optimistic newspaper assessment of this event, the joint communiqué issued at the end of the meeting "represents a commonly agreed choice of areas in which regional co-operation would be possible and would effectively help the countries individually."[16] Though hopeful about the potential benefits of cooperation, other commentators noted that each country appeared to have varying priorities from the outset and that bilateral relations needed to be strengthened first before multilateral cooperation could be expected. For instance, A. S. Abraham, a respected newspaper commentator in India, expressed concern that in identifying areas of cooperation "the seven South Asian countries are putting the cart before the horse. They are seeking a wider co-operation without first devising and strengthening narrower, bilateral ones."[17] Similarly, Neville de Silva, a prominent Sri Lankan journalist, hoped that the 1981 foreign secretaries' meeting in Colombo would enhance regional cooperation, though he warned that "what is ultimately required for successful co-operation is the political will. Without that all the hopes and plans will remain just pious platitudes."[18]

The initial steps for the identification of areas for regional cooperation appeared to be promising, primarily because SAARC undertook to evaluate a concrete range of critical issues that could be addressed at a regional level. Nevertheless, at the first foreign secretaries' meeting it was agreed that a Committee of the Whole (comprised of high-level officials from seven South Asian countries) would be set up to identify other potential areas for collaboration. The first meeting of the Committee of the Whole met in Colombo on 31 August–2 September 1981, just a few months after the inaugural foreign secretaries' meeting. According to Sumit Ganguly, the chief weakness of the Committee of the Whole was that "though composed of senior officials from all seven countries, was seen as a consultative and not a deliberative body. Accordingly, its report stated that final decisions on all issues would be taken by the Foreign Secretaries."[19] During the meeting of the Committee of the Whole, 13 areas of cooperation were identified:

- education and training;
- cultural exchanges;
- scientific and technological cooperation, including new and renewable energy;

- tourism;
- transport;
- shipping;
- monetary cooperation;
- international economic issues;
- information technology and mass communication;
- environment protection;
- policy coordination on manpower;
- NGOs; and
- academic research.

In my view, the 1981 Committee of the Whole meeting represented a turning point—for the wrong reasons—in regional collaboration. The expansion of the number of areas for collaboration announced at the 1981 meeting of the Committee of the Whole signaled the intention of South Asian leaders to address issues of potential collaboration well beyond their capacity to tackle them at a practical level. By the time that SAARC was created in 1985, the association would already have been saddled with a diffuse range of areas for collaboration, thereby sapping the fledgling institution of its possible effectiveness.

## The integrated program of action

A second meeting of South Asian foreign secretaries took place on 1–2 November 1981 in Kathmandu, Nepal, where the report of the five study groups (from the first foreign secretaries' meeting) was accepted. At the session, study groups were upgraded to Working Groups and they were provided with a mandate to draft a comprehensive IPA, a document that over the years has become a core constituent component of the SAARC process.[20] The foreign secretaries agreed that three new areas (from the 13 proposed by the Committee of the Whole) should be added. They included transport, postal services, and scientific and technical cooperation. Subsequently, a third foreign secretaries' meeting took place on 7–9 August 1982 in Islamabad, Pakistan. At this meeting, yet again, new areas for regional cooperation were incorporated: sports, art, and culture. In addition, in order to identify new areas for cooperation, the delegates proposed that a ministerial-level meeting should take place between May and September 1983. On the basis of reports from the Working Groups, a Committee of the Whole was established to draft the IPA, a document that would incorporate all the issues that had been identified as areas for regional collaboration.

The Committee of the Whole eventually met, ahead of schedule, on 10–13 January 1983 in Colombo, the location of the inaugural 1981 South Asian foreign secretaries' meeting. At that stage, there were eight Working Groups operating within this emerging framework of regional collaboration, each struggling to identify short- and long-term targets for cooperation.[21] The short-term action programs identified for cooperation included proposals for the exchange of data, exchange of services by regional experts, and the holding of regional seminars. Long-term action programs included the proposal for the establishment of regional institutions for training and research and the strengthening of physical infrastructure. According to press reports, the Committee of the Whole was concerned "with reviewing already recommended arrangements for co-operative action at a sectoral level, in agreed areas, and with itself recommending arrangements for inter-sectoral co-ordination as well as for the progressive expansion of the areas of co-operative action."[22] Nevertheless, the most important development of the 1983 Committee of the Whole meeting was the presentation of an initial draft of the IPA.

The IPA has since become the focal point for the identification of any additional areas for possible collaboration within the SAARC framework. Clearly, the expanding list of identified issues prompted the need for an additional institutional layer to provide internal coherence and to encourage the implementation of SAARC initiatives. To this effect, Working Groups were redesignated as Technical Committees during the fourth meeting of foreign secretaries held on 28–30 March 1983 in Dhaka, Bangladesh. The idea, in theory, behind this development was that Technical Committees would provide long-term and sustainable expertise to the SAARC secretary general.

A formal declaration on the IPA with areas of cooperation was adopted during the first meeting of South Asian foreign ministers held in New Delhi, India, on 1 August 1983.[23] Building upon the institutional layer provided by the creation of a Technical Committee, the foreign ministers proposed the creation of a permanent Standing Committee comprised of all South Asian foreign secretaries. At the time of the creation of the Standing Committee there was a lack of clarity about its actual purpose. Therefore, in order to identify this, several meetings of the Standing Committee took place.

During the first session of the Standing Committee on 27–29 February 1984 in New Delhi, the work of the Technical Committees was reviewed. In addition, financial arrangements and the world economic situation were discussed. Shortly afterwards, a second session was held in Malé, Maldives, on 7–8 July 1984. There, additional discussions took place regarding SAARC's financial arrangements. Moreover, a review of the implementation of the IPA took place. However, the momentum for developing a set of objectives for adoption by the Standing Committee was derailed following the postponement of the third session of the committee, which had been scheduled to take place on 5–7 February 1985 in Malé, owing to the absence of the necessary number of attendees to form a quorum. Subsequently, a fourth session of the Standing Committee took place on 10–11 May 1985 in Thimpu, Bhutan. However, this meeting was marred by a unilateral boycott by the government of Sri Lanka. Sri Lanka's president Jayewardene objected to comments made by Minister of State for External Affairs, Kurshid Alam Khan, in India's upper legislative chamber, about the ongoing ethnic turmoil in Sri Lanka. In response to Kurshid Alam Khan's critical comments, the government of Sri Lanka decided not to send its foreign secretary to Bhutan. After intense negotiation, Sri Lanka eventually relented and sent a two-man team of senior presidential political advisors to the meeting. According to one observer, "Colombo's non-representation obviously created a tense situation for the first time in the history of SAARC."[24]

The controversy surrounding the fourth session of the Standing Committee in Bhutan signaled that apparently minor bilateral disagreements could disrupt the basic formulation of cooperative arrangements within a South Asian institutional framework. Commenting optimistically on the outcome of the fourth session of the Standing Committee, Pramod Kumar Mishra pointed out that "one of the striking features of the Thimpu meeting was that there was hardly any note of dissent among the participating states on the broader issue of regional cooperation in South Asia."[25] However, at that stage in the institutionalization of SAARC it was unclear what the precise dimensions of the IPA were, what the Technical Committees could do to promote regional collaboration, and what the objectives of the Standing Committee would be in terms of coordinating the activities of the Technical Committees.

Rather than providing clarity to the Standing Committee's own objectives, the foreign secretaries attending the fourth session of the Standing Committee instead opted to finalize a draft Charter for a South Asian regional organization. The Standing Committee agreed that further developments on this fledgling institution should be made at the ministerial level. To this effect, a second meeting of South Asia's foreign ministers was held in Malé on 10–11 July 1984. At the meeting, the ministers agreed to hold the first summit of the association (then tentatively known as the South Asian Regional Cooperation—SARC) in Dhaka at the end of 1985.[26] South Asia's foreign ministers discussed the proposed association's operational activities, but failed to provide clear guidance on the IPA, the existing Technical Committees, or the objectives of the Standing Committee. In the absence of concrete decisions being made by South Asia's foreign ministers at the Malé meeting, a third follow-up foreign ministers' meeting took place in Thimpu, on 13–14 May 1985. The foreign ministers stressed the need for specific projects, but failed to provide any such tangible initiatives. Instead, South Asia's foreign ministers agreed to record a precise date to be set for the first summit of SAARC to be recorded.

The continuing debates about the number of issues that SAARC could agree upon generated some skepticism about the viability of the institution itself. In a provocative article written on the eve of the first SAARC summit, Muhammed Shamshul Huq, a former Bangladeshi foreign minister and chair of the Board of Governors of the Bangladesh Institute of International and Strategic Studies (BIISS) asked some pertinent questions. He asked whether SAARC, "limited to nine areas of cooperation which are of peripheral importance [could] produce any meaningful cooperation with the desired impact on inter-state relations?"[27] He also enquired whether "any significant progress [can] be made even in this limited area of regional cooperation until the resolution of the major bilateral problems?"[28] Finally, he asked whether "viable cooperation [can] be expected to grow among the countries so disparate in their size, population, resource endowment, and stage and pattern of economic growth?"[29]

On 3 December 1985, five foreign secretaries (excluding those from India and Pakistan) held an informal meeting to set up a drafting committee to sort out the proposed amendments and suggestions received from the members on the draft declaration of SARC. The Drafting Committee, headed by Bangladesh, presented its report at the foreign secretaries' meeting on 4 December 1985. According to press reports, Bangladesh's foreign minister, Humayun Rasheed Choudhury, anticipated "a lot of discussions on Afghanistan and Kampuchea."[30] During the fifth session of the Standing Committee, which met on 4 December 1985 in Dhaka, much preparatory work for the first SAARC summit was carried out. After years of wavering over precise details, specific proposals for the streamlining of the process of implementation of the IPA were made. The Standing Committee also stressed that inter-sectoral priorities should be highlighted in the draft Charter. Shortly afterwards, a draft declaration of SAARC was offered for the foreign secretaries' approval. In due course, the session endorsed the Charter and approved the draft declaration. However, special political issues (e.g., Afghanistan and Kampuchea) were not included in the draft declaration. Abul Ahsan, the SARC summit spokesman and Chairman of the

Drafting Committee of the SAARC Declaration, stressed that "no specific political issues" were discussed at the meeting.[31]

The example of regional cooperation in South Asia suggests that the dynamics of regional cooperation do not necessarily represent, at this stage, converging domestic policy preferences among regional states. Instead it appears that SAARC's preference for avoiding discussion about controversial subjects has prompted it to embrace a growing number of areas of possible collaboration within the framework of the IPA. Since 1992, however, the association has gradually moved to attempt to streamline this list and to support a mechanism that will lead to a more effective implementation of SAARC initiatives.[32]

At a formal level, Technical Committees were designed for the purpose of coordinating the work identified in the IPA as areas of cooperation. Each Technical Committee oversees one of the issues in the IPA.[33] At one point, SAARC's IPA had identified up to 17 areas of collaboration, which was clearly an unsustainable number. Over time, the number of issues has decreased, mostly by merging and incorporating them within one Technical Committee. For instance, two separate areas supervised by two separate Technical Committees (e.g., agriculture and rural development) were merged into one Technical Committee. Likewise, the issue of women in development was absorbed into the issue on social development. It remains unclear whether repackaging these Technical Committees has enhanced their effectiveness.

The most notable revamping of the IPA took place in January 2000, when the number of Technical Committees was reduced to incorporate seven areas (namely, agriculture and rural development; communications and transport; energy; environment, meteorology, and forestry; human resources development; social development; and science and technology). In addition, the restructured IPA provides a mechanism whereby the secretary general is expected to report to the Standing Committee on the progress of the implementation of SAARC initiatives stemming from the IPA. In general, despite efforts to improve the operationalization of the IPA, the framing of South Asian collaboration within the context of an IPA remains a contested subject among critics of the association. One keen observer of SAARC, Mahendra P. Lama, points to the fluctuating number of issues included in the IPA and argues that "one can cite several instances of deliberate inaction."[34]

## Collaboration on human capital and social infrastructure

In the previous chapter, I discussed SAARC agreements on a range of security and trade-related issues. As Box 4.1 shows, the majority of

SAARC initiatives deal with such matters. The differential rate between the signing of security and trade-specific agreements and conventions also suggests that SAARC member states are eager to collaborate in those areas where the expected gains from collaboration are greatest and not based on areas where agreement can be reached most swiftly. Paradoxically, SAARC member states have reached more tangible agreements on issues (e.g., security, trade) that were not explicitly identified as an area

***Box 4.1*** **SAARC principles and major initiatives**

***Principles***

- Adherence to the principles of sovereign equality, territorial integrity and national independence
- Renunciation of the use or threat of force
- Non-interference in the internal affairs of other member-states
- Peaceful settlement of all disputes
- Cooperation among member states to enhance prosperity of and stability in the region

***Major initiatives***

- SAARC Regional Convention on suppression of terrorism, Kathmandu, 4 November 1987
- SAARC Convention on narcotic drugs and psychotropic substances, Malé, 3 November 1990
- SAARC Convention on preventing and combating trafficking in women and children for prostitution, Kathmandu, 5 January 2002
- SAARC Convention on regional arrangements for the promotion of child welfare in South Asia, Kathmandu, 5 January 2002
- Agreement on the South Asia Free Trade Area (SAFTA), Islamabad, 6 January 2004
- Agreement for the establishment of the SAARC Arbitration Council, Dhaka, 13 November 2005
- SAARC limited multilateral agreement on avoidance of double taxation and mutual administrative assistance in tax matters, Dhaka, 13 November 2005
- SAARC Agreement on mutual administrative assistance in customs matters, Dhaka, 13 November 2005
- Agreement on establishing the SAARC Food Bank, New Delhi, 3 April 2007

- SAARC Development Fund, Colombo, 3 August 2008
- SAARC Convention on mutual assistance in criminal matters, Colombo, 3 August 2008
- Agreement on the establishment of South Asian Regional Standards Organisation (SARSO), Colombo, 3 August 2008

Source: Extracted from the South Asian Association for Regional Cooperation website (available at www.saarc-sec.org).

of collaboration in the IPA or for which there was no existing Technical Committee to promote collaboration.

Nevertheless, it would be unfair to isolate SAARC agreements on security and trade-related matters as being the sole evidence for the success of the SAARC mechanism for regional collaboration. SAARC has been a leader on the promotion of human resource development and social infrastructure. The strong institutional commitment to development was first voiced at the summit declaration of the first SAARC summit. In that declaration, SAARC member states pointed to South Asia's potential in terms of being a "huge market, their substantial human and natural resources and the complementarities of their economies." SAARC member states also expressed the view that "they were confident that with effective regional cooperation, they could make optimum use of these capacities for the benefit of their peoples, accelerate the pace of their economic development and enhance their national and collective self-reliance."[35] Since then, SAARC has reiterated this message with increasing specificity on areas of human resource development, particularly in terms of sports, arts and culture.

Since its creation, SAARC has also attempted to coordinate the guidance provided by the ever-changing IPA while at the same time funneling its focus on a broad range of developmental activities. The initiation of new areas of policy interest has, in recent years, been closely tied to advancement in the achievement of the Millennium Development Goals (MDGs). In terms of SAARC's commitment to development, many of the issues of mutual concern were encapsulated in the SAARC Social Charter, a document signed by all SAARC member states in Islamabad on 6 January 2004. In the SAARC Social Charter, member states pledged to "maintain a social policy and strategy in order to ensure an overall and balanced social development of their peoples" and to "establish a people-centered framework for social development to guide their work and in the future, to build a culture of cooperation and partnership and to respond to the immediate needs of those who are most affected by human distress."[36]

The 2004 SAARC Social Charter set out a range of commitments relating to developmental activities, particularly those focusing on poverty alleviation, health, human resource development, promotion of the status of women, population stabilization, and child welfare. Regional cooperation on some of these issues had already resulted in the signing of the 2002 SAARC convention on regional arrangements for the promotion of child welfare in South Asia and the 2002 SAARC convention on preventing and combating trafficking in women and children for prostitution. Moreover, the 2004 Social Charter attempted to provide support to existing development funding mechanisms. Prior to the signing of the Charter, SAARC had established the South Asian Development Fund (SADF). The SADF merged two small existing funding mechanisms, the SAARC Fund for Regional Projects and the SAARC Regional Fund.

The purpose of the SADF had been ambitious, principally to support industrial development, poverty alleviation, protection of the environment, human resource development, and promotion of social and infrastructure development projects in the SAARC region. To that effect, the SADF pooled resources from SAARC member states, with a starting budget of US $5 million. During the initial stages of the SADF's operation, SAARC member states also considered the idea of funding sectoral developmental projects, principally through the creation of a Poverty Alleviation Fund, Infrastructure Fund, South Asian Development Bank, Media Development Fund, and a Voluntary Fund for the Differently Able Persons. In practice, though, the SADF fell short of its stated development objectives. Although its funding eventually increased to US $7 million, the SADF was eventually dissolved in June 2008. According to my interviews at the SAARC Secretariat, the achievements of the SADF, from its inception in 1996 until 2008, amounted to the completion of 16 feasibility studies.

The failure of the SADF did not deter SAARC member states from implementing the 2004 SAARC Social Charter through a reconstituted development funding mechanism. At the 13th SAARC summit, held in Dhaka in November 2005, SAARC member states recommended the creation of a new development funding mechanism, to be called the SAARC Development Fund (SDF). The SDF, a reconstituted version of the SADF, was to "serve as the umbrella financial institution for all SAARC projects and programmes."[37] Based on the proposal made by

SAARC member states in the 13th summit declaration, the SDF would acquire a permanent secretariat and divide its functions along three areas or "windows," namely a Social Window, an Infrastructure Window, and an Economic Window.

A SAARC Development Fund Charter was drawn up and ratified, and subsequently the SDF was formally announced during the 16th SAARC summit declaration signed on 29 April 2010 in Thimpu. SAARC member states highlighted the critical importance of appropriate development funding, but were cognizant that a SAARC-led development fund needed to have tangible performance outputs. They urged the importance of projects being funded through the SDF as being "demand-driven, time-bound and aligned with the developmental priorities of the region."[38] Thus, from an institutional perspective, the most concrete outcome of the SAARC Social Charter has been the reconstitution of a faltering development funding mechanism, the SADF, and the creation of a reconstituted development funding mechanism, the SDF.

During the early years of SAARC, though, the more substantial human resource development theme left unaddressed by the association's member states was that of education. At the fourth SAARC summit held in Islamabad in December 1988, the heads of state and government agreed for the first time to incorporate education as an area of cooperation. One could argue that SAARC member states should have attributed greater significance to this issue at an earlier date. Even though the largest contribution to the GDP of South Asian economies are services (rather than agriculture or manufacturing), it is a region where economic growth is hampered by low literacy rates and low levels of investment in education. As Table 4.1 shows, at the time of the fourth SAARC summit, the overall levels of literacy for South Asian countries were low—particularly among women—as were levels of educational expenditure.

Table 4.1 shows that overall literacy in the Maldives and Sri Lanka is exceptionally high, particularly as they are low-income economies. However, at the time of the fourth SAARC summit, literacy rates were very low for Bangladesh and Nepal, slightly over 35 percent and 32 percent, respectively.[39] On a more promising note, the literacy rates for youth were slightly higher, in some cases nearly 10 percentage points higher than for overall adult literacy rates. This fact is quite important because the demographic distribution in South Asia is heavily skewed to people under 25 years of age. Nearly 50 percent of the population in most South Asian countries is under 25 years of age.[40]

The data on literacy rates for women in Table 4.1 are far more worrisome. In general, female literacy rates are 10 percentage points lower than for the overall population. At the time of the fourth SAARC

*Table 4.1* Basic statistics on literacy and public spending on education, 1989–1999

| | *Literacy rate, adult total (%)* | *Literacy rate, youth total (% of people, ages 15–24)* | *Literacy rate, women total (% of people, ages 15 and above)* | *Public spending on education total (% GDP)* |
|---|---|---|---|---|
| Bangladesh | 35.3 | 44.7 | 25.8 | 2.4 |
| Bhutan | n.a. | n.a. | n.a. | 5.8 |
| India | 48.2 | 61.9 | 33.7 | 4.4 |
| Maldives | 96.1 | 98.1 | 96.4 | 3.7 |
| Nepal | 32.9 | 49.6 | 17.4 | 2.9 |
| Pakistan | 42.7 | 55.3 | 29.1 | 2.6 |
| Sri Lanka | 90.7 | 95.5 | 89.1 | 3.1 |

Source: United Nations Educational, Scientific and Cultural Organization.

summit, the female literacy rates for Bangladesh, Nepal, and Pakistan were very low (under 30 percent), and far below the overall literacy rates. More alarmingly, there were substantial disparities between the female literacy rates in urban and rural settings.[41] Nevertheless, the problem of low female literacy is not unique to Bangladesh, Nepal or Pakistan. Female literacy rates for India were not much higher during the same period. In contrast, the Maldives and Sri Lanka achieved high literacy levels among women, almost equivalent to literacy rates in the whole population.

Moreover, Table 4.1 shows that the level of public expenditure on education varies quite considerably across South Asia. Data on public expenditure on education consists of current and capital public expenditure, including government spending on educational institutions (both public and private), education administration and subsidies for private entities (students/households and other private entities). The macrolevel data in Table 4.1 shows that Bhutan, India, the Maldives, and Sri Lanka have the highest levels of public investment in education, with rates that are equivalent to educational expenditures in high-income Asian countries.[42] Although it would be erroneous to draw the conclusion that higher education expenditures automatically lead to higher literacy levels, it is clear that underinvestment in education—particularly in the cases of Bangladesh, Nepal, and Pakistan—has not translated into spectacular literacy rates, particularly for women.

To this effect, SAARC has attempted to voice its concern about the policy implications of low literacy rates for women in South Asia. For instance, on 8 May 1986 a ministerial meeting on the subject of women in development met in Shillong, India, and issued a joint communiqué which suggested that "greater attention was needed towards the low rate of literacy, poor vocational training, [and the] low level of political awareness and the quality of life particularly in rural areas needs attention."[43] In order to implement specific activities to address this concern, SAARC established a Technical Committee on Women in Development. However, at the second SAARC summit, held in Bangalore, India, on 16–17 November 1986, the issue of women in development as a priority of human resource development got sidetracked in favor of a competing concern, namely the needs of children. The 1986 SAARC summit declaration stated that "meeting the needs of all children was the principal means of human resources development. Children should, therefore, be given the highest priority in national development planning."[44] Eventually, SAARC decided to nominate 2001–10 as the Decade of the Child.

This is not to imply that SAARC abandoned its commitment to the issue of women in development. The SAARC Technical Committee on Women in Development attempted to draw attention to issues relating to the status of women in South Asia. According to one analysis of the committee's work, "one of the most important features of the work of the Technical Committee was designating 1990 as SAARC Year of Girl Child and 1991–2000 as the SAARC Decade of the Girl Child."[45] Nevertheless, in January 2000, the Technical Committee on Women in Development was merged within a more general Technical Committee on Development. The Technical Committee on Development met once but shortly thereafter was disbanded. It appears that increasingly SAARC began to link the issue of women in development with policy issues relating to children. For instance, on 5 January 2002, SAARC signed a convention on preventing and combating trafficking in women and children for prostitution. In January 2004, a new Technical Committee on Women, Children, and Youth was created. At present, apart from the 2002 convention preventing and combating trafficking in women and children for prostitution, the most concrete SAARC modality and mechanism for implementation, coordination, and monitoring of women in South Asia has been the creation of the SAARC Gender Info Base (SGIB), an agency that provides information and operates in tandem with the SAARC Secretariat and the United Nations Development Fund for Women (UNIFEM).[46]

South Asia's statistics on education pose a fundamental developmental challenge to South Asian economies, specifically as it relates to human capital. Building on the pioneering work on human capital undertaken by Jacob Mincer, subsequent studies have shown a positive relationship between educational attainment and income levels as well as between education and economic growth.[47] Thus, it has increasingly become a truism that improvements in educational outcomes should lead to positive consequences in economic growth. Accordingly, investment in social infrastructure, particularly education, should normatively be one of the principal aims of SAARC.

SAARC's implementation of collaboration agreements on education has been encouraging, albeit long delayed and with little concrete evidence of significant policy outputs. For instance, following the 10th SAARC summit held in Colombo in July 1998, the vice-chancellors of the open universities of SAARC member states agreed to the establishment of a SAARC Consortium on Open and Distance Learning (SACODiL). At present, four institutions are members of the SACODiL consortium. They consist of the Bangladesh Open University, Indira Gandhi Open University, Allama Iqbal Open University, and the Open University of Sri Lanka. Nevertheless, despite some initial enthusiasm, actual implementation of distance learning in South Asia under the auspices of SACODiL has been slow. Since the 10th SAARC summit, members of the SACODiL consortium have agreed to set up a rotational secretariat and to establish a board of governors. The first meeting of the SACODiL board of governors took place in January 2005 in New Delhi. But it was not until the third meeting of the SACODiL board of governors in February 2007 in Islamabad that specific proposals on distance learning and network collaboration were drafted.

A more exciting development pertaining to SAARC collaboration on education was the creation of the South Asian University. During the 13th SAARC summit held in Dhaka in November 2005, India's prime minister Manmohan Singh proposed for the first time the creation of a SAARC-supported university that would host students and researchers from South Asia. The proposal itself received little attention in the press and in the official declaration of the Dhaka summit. Within the context of a broad discussion on South Asia's agenda on social issues, the 2005 SAARC summit declaration merely stated that SAARC member states "noted the offer of India to establish a South Asian University and agreed to examine this matter further."[48]

Under normal circumstances, the strength of such diplomatic language would lead one to believe that little or no direct action would follow this proposal.[49] However, at the 14th SAARC summit held in New Delhi in April 2007, the member states signed an inter-governmental agreement for the establishment of the South Asian University. The text of the SAARC declaration of the 13th summit provided an ambitious overview of the goals of the 2007 inter-governmental agreement. The declaration mentioned that SAARC member states "further directed that the Intergovernmental Steering Committee be set up at the earliest [opportunity] to complete its tasks relating to the Charter, bye laws, rules and regulations, curriculum development, business plans and other issues. They also decided to strengthen cooperation and dialogue on educational matters through development of exchanges between academics, experts, policymakers, students and teachers."[50]

The signing of the agreement per se could have been considered an important achievement by SAARC, but what was surprising was the fact that implementation of this proposal was quickly pursued through domestic legislative channels. Draft legislation for the establishment of the South Asian University was introduced in both chambers of the Indian parliament (the Lok Sabha and the Rajya Sabha) and final bills were approved during the 14th session of the Lok Sabha in December 2008. The unusually swift approval of the South Asian University Bill (2008) in the Lok Sabha signaled that there was widespread political support for this project and, accordingly, the Indian government could act speedily to bring the university to fruition. During the implementation stage, Manmohan Singh also secured funding to acquire land and oversee construction in New Delhi. The temporary campus, located in South Delhi, opened for teaching in August 2010.

Although other SAARC member states have provided some financial assistance, the Indian government has provided the bulk of the start-up costs of the university. It is estimated that nearly 50 percent of the overall costs will be borne by India, at least until 2014. For its part, the establishment of the university raised a number of important sensitive issues, including the exact budgetary contribution by each SAARC member state, and the appointment of a rotating chancellor of the university. First and foremost, though, was the proposition that the establishment of the university would necessitate improvements in the visa regime for students and researchers traveling within South Asia. Discussions about such improvements in the visa regime took place at a time when diplomatic relations between India and Pakistan were at a standstill, following the November 2008 terrorist attacks in Mumbai, India. Despite the tense diplomatic standoff, India responded to Pakistani governmental complaints about a proposed differential treatment for Pakistani staff and students attending the South Asian University. In May 2010, India's Ministry of the Interior announced that it had altered its visa regime to enable Pakistani staff and students enrolled at the South Asian University to enjoy the same visa regime as other foreign staff and students based in Indian universities.[51]

The establishment of the South Asian University offers important lessons for future collaboration in South Asia. First, it signals that SAARC can be an effective forum for the initiation of important projects that could have beneficial multilateral effects. The swift establishment of the South Asian University, though, also shows that SAARC's existing institutional mechanism for filtering out issues that could be deemed to be controversial or bilateral in nature is too timorous and is likely to discourage fruitful engagement in South Asia. A third important lesson has been that South Asian collaboration can take place even if India exercises a leadership role. A fourth lesson that may be derived from this experience is that India and Pakistan *can* collaborate, even in the midst of very tense bilateral relations.[52] In general, these lessons should motivate SAARC to be more adventurous in encouraging individual states to initiate the promotion of regional cooperation.

## SAARC regional centers, apex and recognized bodies

An organic development in the way that SAARC has attempted to facilitate regional collaboration has been through the development of SAARC regional centers.[53] During the first session of the Council of Ministers held in Dhaka on 12–13 August 1987, the establishment of a SAARC Meteorological Research Center was proposed. In parallel, the Technical Committee on Agriculture fomented the idea of setting up a SAARC Agricultural Information Center. This was established in Dhaka in 1988.

Since the creation of the SAARC Agricultural Information Center (SAIC), eight other regional centers have been established. In general, SAARC regional centers can be split into two functional areas: those that engage in collaborative research and training and those that engage in knowledge transfer as information provision hubs (see Table 4.2).

Viewed from an optimistic angle, SAARC regional centers arguably provide the most tangible basis for regional collaboration on pragmatic issues and can be regarded as a successful outcome of collaboration between SAARC member states. However, their performance has been lacking. For instance, the report of the SAARC group of eminent persons offered a dire assessment of the quality of the SAARC regional centers. According to the SAARC-sponsored committee report, none of the SAARC regional centers "have emerged as recognized centers of excellence in the region. They have bogged down to routine activities and are hardly distinguishable from the national centers with which they are associated."[54]

Structurally the regional centers are supposed to operate under the purview of a SAARC Working Division. Thematically they could be seen as an offshoot of stated areas of cooperation as specified in the IPA. However, there is an existing asymmetry between the stated areas of cooperation and the structure of the SAARC Secretariat and the SAARC

*Table 4.2* SAARC regional centers, 1985–2010

| *SAARC regional center* | *Acronym* | *Location* | *Year of inauguration* |
|---|---|---|---|
| SAARC Agricultural Information Center | SAIC | Dhaka, Bangladesh | 1985 |
| SAARC Meteorological Research Center | SMRC | Dhaka, Bangladesh | 1995 |
| SAARC Energy Center | SEC | Islamabad, Pakistan | 2006 |
| SAARC Coastal Zone Management Center | SCZMC | Malé, Maldives | 2005 |
| SAARC Human Resources Development Center | SHRDC | Islamabad, Pakistan | 2002 |
| SAARC Documentation Center | SDC | New Delhi, India | 1994 |
| SAARC Information Center | SIC | Kathmandu, Nepal | 2008 |
| SAARC Disaster Management Center | SDMC | New Delhi, India | 2006 |
| SAARC Tuberculosis and HIV/Aids Center | STC | Kathmandu, Nepal | 1992 |
| SAARC Forestry Center | SFC | Thimpu, Bhutan | 2008 |
| SAARC Cultural Center | SCC | Sri Lanka | under development |

Source: SAARC Secretariat.

regional centers. As discussed in Chapter 1, there have been as many as 17 areas of cooperation, eight SAARC Secretariat Working Divisions, and nine SAARC regional centers. Each Working Division, however, is responsible for areas that may have little policy connection to each other (e.g., energy, tourism, and science). The inclusion of Afghanistan as a member state has led to the creation of an Afghanistan-specific Working Division (i.e., media and integration of Afghanistan).

As Table 4.3 shows, some Working Divisions have no corresponding regional center. This situation illustrates that there is an inherent disconnection between the institutional structure of the SAARC Secretariat's Working Divisions and the regional centers, resulting in a patchwork of secondary institutions to assist the Secretariat.

Another feature of the institutional structure of this regional body is the presence of various layers of secondary institutions. One such layer is the SAARC Working Groups. Existing Working Groups are expected to work closely with a SAARC Working Division corresponding with their thematic area. Working Groups are also expected to formulate, coordinate, evaluate, and oversee programs as directed by other higher

*Table 4.3* Relationship between SAARC Working Divisions and SAARC regional centers

| *SAARC Working Division* | *SAARC regional center* |
|---|---|
| Agriculture and rural development | SAARC Agricultural Information Center |
| Economy, trade, and finance | [No corresponding thematic regional center] |
| Energy, tourism, and science | SAARC Energy Center |
| Environment and biotechnology | SAARC Meteorological Research Center, SAARC Disaster Management Center, SAARC Coastal Zone Management Center, SAARC Forestry Center |
| Human resource development, security, and culture | SAARC Human Resources Development Center |
| Information and poverty alleviation | SAARC Documentation Center, SAARC Information Center |
| Media and integration of Afghanistan | SAARC Information Center |
| Social affairs | SAARC Tuberculosis and HIV/Aids Center |

Source: SAARC Secretariat.

SAARC bodies (principally the SAARC Secretariat, SAARC Council of Ministers, the SAARC Standing Committee, and the SAARC Technical Committees). At present, there are four SAARC Working Groups. These include: the Working Group on Biotechnology, the Working Group in Energy, the Working Group on Information and Communication Technology, and a Working Group on Tourism. Aside from the absence of a presence at the regional level, there is no clear distinction between SAARC Working Groups and SAARC regional centers. However, there appears to be a pattern whereby some SAARC regional centers start off as SAARC Working Groups.

An additional institutional layer for facilitating regional cooperation is constituted by SAARC apex and recognized bodies. SAARC apex bodies are, in essence, regional non-governmental organizations (NGOs) that work in close collaboration to support people-to-people contacts. These institutions are registered with the SAARC Secretariat, but there is no financial obligation for SAARC to support SAARC apex bodies. Arguably the most active SAARC apex body is the SCCI. The SCCI is an umbrella organization that brings together the various chambers of commerce among SAARC member states. Much of its work is devoted to organizing trade fairs, promoting trade delegations within South

Asia, and publishing useful reports on economic cooperation in South Asia. More importantly, its lobbying work on behalf of closer economic and trade ties was instrumental in fostering the development of the SAPTA.

Other existing SAARC apex bodies include the South Asian Association for Regional Co-operation in Law (SAARCLAW), the South Asian Federation of Accountants (SAFA), the South Asia Foundation, and the Foundation of SAARC Writers and Literature. These associations have been helpful in promoting regional expertise on given areas. For instance, SAARCLAW is an association that has sponsored a large number of conferences that bring together lawyers, judges, and legal scholars.

In addition to the SAARC apex bodies, another institutional layer for member countries are the SAARC recognized bodies.[55] SAARC recognized bodies are regional professional bodies whose aim is to foster cooperation and to promote coordinated regional action and consultation of key policy matters. Like SAARC apex bodies, these institutions are registered with the SAARC Secretariat and they also receive no financial support from the association. Nevertheless, since the establishment of the first SAARC recognized body, the Association of Management and Development Institutions in South Asia (AMDISA), there has been a rapid proliferation of SAARC recognized bodies. At present these include: SAARC Association of Town Planners, South Asian Federation of Accountants (SAFA), SAARC Federation of University Women (SAARCFUW), South Asian Association for Regional Cooperation of Architects (SAARCH), Federation of State Insurance Organizations of SAARC Countries (FSIO), SAARC Diploma Engineers Forum (SDEF), Radiological Society of SAARC Countries (RSSC), SAARC Teachers Federation (STF), SAARC Surgical Care Society (SSCS), South Asian Regional Association of Dermatologists, Venereologists and Leprologists (SARAD), South Asian Free Media Association (SAFMA), SAARC Women's Association in Sri Lanka (SWA), Hindukush Himalayan Grassroots Women's Natural Resources Management (HIMAWANTI), Federation of Association of Pediatric Surgeons of SAARC Countries (FAPSS), South Asian Federation of Exchanges (SAFE), Association of SAARC Speakers and Parliamentarians, SAARC Cardiac Society, and the SAARC Federation of Oncologists (SFO).

Based on the sprawling nature of the SAARC institutions and issue areas (as well as SAARC's own poor record of achievement), one might be tempted to dismiss the importance of SAARC apex and recognized bodies. However, their proliferation points to an important development, namely the process of a shared regional identity that does not rest exclusively on a common colonial heritage. Moreover, these institutions serve a functional purpose. SAARC recognized bodies, in particular, have helped to promote expertise and professional links across different South Asian countries, particularly in areas where there is a substantial need for capacity building. Given that the share of services as a proportion of gross domestic product is very high in these low-income countries, any effort to support trade in services can only be beneficial to South Asian economies.

## Conclusion

As I have shown in this chapter, there has been a considerable increase in the number of issues identified at various foreign secretaries' meetings. However, there is no corresponding institutional structure within the aegis of SAARC that could identify areas of possible cooperation. In a frank assessment by a former SAARC secretary general on the difficulties of cooperation in South Asia under the SAARC framework, Ibrahim Hussain Zaki observed that "political differences and bilateral disputes between member countries tend to bear an inhibiting effect on the political will of South Asian leaders to move beyond the rhetoric of regional cooperation."[56]

In the absence of an enforcement mechanism to guarantee compliance, regional cooperation can only exist to the extent that participants agree *ab initio*. During interviews which I undertook at the SAARC Secretariat and regional centers, it became clear, though, that the real difficulty for SAARC lies at the implementation stage of agreements and conventions. The SAARC regional conventions and agreements are a first step to encourage SAARC member states to enact legislation that makes it possible for individual agreements and conventions to be implemented. The introduction of domestic law into the implementation of SAARC initiatives is the single greatest challenge to the effectiveness of SAARC. Since the implementation of SAARC initiatives requires unanimous consent from the domestic regulatory bodies of all member states, then any single country can act as an effective veto on SAARC effectiveness.

It may be reasonable to anticipate that in order for SAARC to be more effective, it will have to abandon its founding principle of requiring unanimity in decision-making and the explicit avoidance of controversial subjects. While the principle of unanimity may have been useful during the institution-building phase of SAARC, it now inhibits true collaboration beyond a rather superficial common front.

# 5 Future challenges

- Types of regional integration
- Challenges of membership and enlargement
- Challenges to security stability
- Challenges to social and developmental integration

In this chapter I will examine some of the problems laid out throughout this book as well as fundamental challenges that SAARC will face in the future.[1] One could argue that many of the problems that this regional body has faced in the past result from an impoverished institutional design during the time of the foundation of the association. As I will discuss below, other problems that SAARC has previously confronted are of a more general nature, namely an absence of strategic vision on the part of the heads of state and government in South Asia.

This critique of the institutional design and strategic vision of SAARC need not be seen as an overall rejection of the aims of the association. On the contrary, we must understand that South Asia is an incredibly complex and turbulent region of the world, so any institution that moves in the direction of promoting regional cooperation should be welcomed.

Throughout this book, we have understood that the association can be credited for some successes, such as the signing of the SAFTA. Some critics could rightly point out that these initiatives have taken too long or that they fall short of an ideal situation. Nevertheless, institutional achievements should be measured on their own terms, taking into account the structural obstacles that the founders of SAARC have put into place in the SAARC Charter. In some respects, such as the creation of the South Asian University, the successes have taken place in spite of the cumbersome internal mechanisms established for the purpose of promoting regional cooperation. On the other hand, though, it is important to assess the future challenges and difficulties that inhibit the association from moving beyond the initial stages of institutionalization and begin overcoming some of the structural obstacles that have prevented it from becoming a more successful beacon of regional collaboration in South Asia.

## Types of regional integration

The literature on comparative regional integration is indebted to the pioneering work of Joseph Nye in providing a typology of different types of integration (i.e., economic, social, and political).[2] One of the assumptions of this typology is that different forms of regional integration can emerge autonomously, but they are constrained by the degree of institutionalization of other forms of regional integration. Moreover, changes to these forms of regional integration flow from the degree of regional institutional coherence. Viewed in this structural context, it remains to be determined what the role of regional institutions, like SAARC, has been in fostering regional integration.

This book has attempted to provide a detailed overview of SAARC, from its genesis through its historical development and current role in South Asia. I have examined the challenges that the association has faced in terms of its expansion and the interest shown by other nations to join up as a full member. I have evaluated the association's efforts to provide a regional security framework and to promote economic collaboration. In addition, I have examined its diffuse efforts to specify a coherent integrated program of action to facilitate regional cooperation in areas outside of security and economic cooperation. Nevertheless, one of the most challenging theoretical and empirical propositions is to determine the link between the growing institutionalization of the association to the increasing levels of regional interdependence that are likely to be taking place in the future in South Asia.

## Challenges of membership and enlargement

In the first 25 years since its establishment, SAARC has only increased its membership by one. In Chapter 2 I showed that Afghanistan was admitted as a member state to this regional body in 2005. It would be unscholarly to predict the future political stability of that country in, say, 25 years' time. Nevertheless, Afghanistan in 2005 was a highly unstable country. It remains very unstable at the time of the writing of this book and there is no apparent evidence that this situation will change any time soon. In the Failed States Index 2010, for instance, Afghanistan ranks number six as the country with the most critical level of stability.[3] According to this measure, Afghanistan's ranking has been increasing on a yearly basis and, for the first time, surpassed Iraq in terms of its overall index score as a failed state.

The inclusion of Afghanistan as a SAARC member state raises important questions for the viability of regional cooperation in South Asia. One should ponder whether a failed state can make an effective member of an association for regional cooperation. As it stands, Afghanistan's participation in SAARC has been circumscribed. The association has a rotating leadership and summit structure, but at present no SAARC summit can take place in Afghanistan until the internal security situation improves dramatically in that country. Afghanistan's participation has also been limited in other perceptible ways. For instance, within the structure of the SAARC Secretariat, there is a Working Division on media and integration of Afghanistan. This is the only Working Division that is country specific. If the objective of regional associations is to foster regional collaboration, then Afghanistan's participation, at present, is incompatible with that aim. Moreover, there is no SAARC regional center or any form of SAARC institutional presence in Afghanistan.

The incorporation of Afghanistan as a member state within this institution raises another uncomfortable prospect. In the absence of an external force to support it, Afghanistan is likely to collapse politically and administratively. Alternatively, Afghanistan could acquire some form of political stability under a Taliban-style regime. It is plausible that such a regime in control of the government of Afghanistan would refuse to participate in a forum for regional cooperation like SAARC. However, there is no evidence to suggest that this could be the case. During the period of Taliban rule in Afghanistan (1996–2001), the Afghan government participated in international institutions, albeit admittedly in a limited fashion. One may want to ask how SAARC should handle a situation whereby the *raison d'être* of one of its member states is inimical to the objectives of the association. Other regional associations have faced this problem, but the case of SAARC is distinctive. First, as stipulated in Article 10.1 of the SAARC Charter, it is an association that operates on the principle of governance through unanimity. The SAARC Charter specifies that "decisions at all levels shall be taken on the basis of unanimity."[4] The association has no existing method for removing the rights of membership to any member state, even in cases where a member state does not contribute to the overall financial arrangements of the association. According to Article 9.1 of the SAARC Charter, "the contribution of each Member State towards financing of the activities of the association shall be voluntary."[5] In other words, there is no mechanism for the expulsion of a member state for non-payment of its dues. Finally, given the association's strict avoidance of the discussion of subjects that may be deemed controversial, then the issue of expelling a member state from this regional body could not be legitimately raised.

The questions raised by the inclusion of a government that would be antagonistic to the overall aims of the association are certainly not limited to Afghanistan. At present, Afghanistan is the most salient example of the impact that the incorporation of a failed state can have on regional cooperation. As early as 2009, several other SAARC member states were deemed to be at risk of being categorized as failed states. In the 2009 Failed States Index, Pakistan was ranked number 10, Bangladesh was ranked number 19, Sri Lanka was ranked number 22, and Nepal was ranked number 25.[6] In total, five out of the eight SAARC member states were deemed to be failed states according to the Failed States Index devised by *Foreign Policy* magazine and the Fund for Peace. Among these countries, the internal security situation has improved as a result of an apparent end to the civil wars in Sri Lanka and Nepal. However, the internal security situation in Pakistan has been consistently precarious.

One may wonder whether the absence of a mechanism to expel or, at least, suspend members from the association is a severe structural obstacle to regional collaboration. In this respect, SAARC should perhaps emulate the AU insofar as members can be suspended from the Union, typically because a government has seized power through a *coup d'état*. For instance, Article 30 of the Constitutive Act of the AU provides that "Governments which shall come to power through unconstitutional means shall not be allowed to participate in the activities of the Union."[7] Moreover, Article 23 of the Constitutive Act of that regional body also provides that member states are subject to sanctions if they default in the payment of their contributions to the budget of the Union.[8] The Constitutive Act of the AU used to include a draconian clause relating to expulsion from that institution. However, this provision of the Constitutive Act has been amended in subsequent protocols.[9]

The question of whether the inclusion of failed states could threaten the viability of regional cooperation is not merely speculative or academic. Prior to attending the 2005 SAARC summit held in Dhaka, Bangladesh, India's prime minister Manmohan Singh made vague references to the threat posed to regional stability by failed states. On the eve of his trip, he gave a speech in which he warned that "the danger of a number of failed States emerging in our neighbourhood has far reaching consequences for our region and our people. The impact includes crises which generate an inflow of refugees and by destabilisation of our border areas."[10] Since the Indian prime minister did not make it clear to which specific countries he was referring, his comments were not well received in other South Asian countries. For instance, a Pakistani newspaper's analysis of Manmohan Singh's controversial statements concluded that although "he did not name any country, he may have been referring to Nepal, where there is Maoist militancy, Bangladesh's recent disturbances, Pakistan's unprecedented earthquake, or Sri Lanka which is facing Tamil insurgency. The purpose of this statement, just a day before his departure for Dhaka to attend the summit, is not understandable."[11]

The question of SAARC membership raises another curious prospect, unlikely to be replicated in other similar institutional settings. Although the Maldives has been politically stable since its independence, the country faces the pressing problem that it could cease to exist as a geographic entity, literally. A report issued by the Maldivian government's Ministry of Home Affairs, Housing and Environment reported that sea levels appear to be rising at a rate of 0.9 centimeters per year.[12] Since the majority of the country's islands are one meter or less above sea level, then the expectation is that most of the inhabited parts of the Maldives could be submerged within the next century. The threat posed by global climate change to low-lying coastal regions and small island states has been highlighted by the United Nations Intergovernmental Panel on Climate Change.[13] Although some independent reports have questioned the degree to which the Maldives are likely to be under threat from such projected increases in flooding, several islands in the Maldives were swallowed by the sea during the 2004 tsunami.[14]

To counteract any possible damage from rising sea levels, the government of the Maldives has made it a key strategic developmental priority to counteract any potential environmental damage caused by global climate change. According to a strategic review undertaken by the office of the President of the Maldives, climate change is a grave security concern "because rising sea levels, for instance, threaten the very existence of many island nations such as Maldives."[15] In the Maldivian government's view, "the country's vulnerability to climate change and sea level rise is evident. Major vulnerabilities identified include severe beach erosion, damage to human health and infrastructure, loss of biodiversity and impacts on food security and the economy."[16] In order to mitigate the most pessimistic scenarios, the government of the Maldives has initiated an aggressive campaign of sustainable adaptation measures and has even investigated the possibility of relocating its population to another part of the world. Obviously one would hope that the Maldives would be able to continue to exist in its current geographic location, but it is not far-fetched to think otherwise. At present, the most viable options appear to be a wholescale relocation of the Maldivian population to India. Under these exceptional circumstances, SAARC should take active steps to provide plans, borne out of regional cooperation, to accommodate the needs of the Maldives.

Finally, SAARC's future challenges relating to membership include the growing interest shown by other institutions in being granted observer status. Some countries that currently enjoy observer status have expressed interest in gaining full membership. In Chapter 2 of this book, I revealed the interest of Myanmar and Iran in becoming full members of the association. These particular requests were made rather indirectly, which may signal a lack of substantive interest on the part of these two countries to join SAARC. The more serious challenge to the current composition of SAARC, though, lies in China's interest in joining as a full member.

## Challenges to security stability

The question of the challenge to regional cooperation on security issues was discussed in greater detail in Chapter 3. As has been suggested, South Asia's security problems have a regional component as well as a domestic dimension.[17] India and Pakistan have been traditional adversaries and therefore the regional dimension of security problems has been dominated by this rivalry. Prior to the creation of SAARC, India and Pakistan fought three wars; the first taking place shortly after the partition of India in 1947, the second in 1965, and the third in 1971. On another front, China and India engaged each other in a border conflict in 1962. China's support for Pakistan after the 1962 Indo-China war added further complexity to the tenuous relationship between India and Pakistan. Viewed in this light, actions by one state are likely to be misinterpreted by its neighbors. According to an analyst of Pakistan's security concerns, for instance, "in Pakistan's security calculations and foreign-policy determinations, India's intentions towards Pakistan are always regarded as malignant."[18]

It is beyond the scope of this book to analyze the causes of these militarized interstate disputes in South Asia, but in general they point to important security consequences for the region, particularly by generating crisis instability. For instance, two years after the creation of SAARC, the Indian Army undertook a large military exercise in the state of Rajasthan, an area bordering Pakistan. The military exercise, codenamed Operation Brasstacks, lasted from November 1986 to March 1987. The five-month deployment of Indian ground troops along the border with Pakistan was interpreted in Pakistani military circles—perhaps understandably—as preparation for an invasion. The Pakistani government reacted to what it considered to be a threat to its security by amassing a large number of troops and armored units to repel a potential invasion by India. That the border standoff did not escalate into a war was a result of intense diplomatic negotiations that took place between India's prime minister Rajiv Gandhi and Pakistan's president Zia-ul-Haq.

Operation Brasstacks revealed that, in the context of the tense relations between India and Pakistan, an otherwise minor incident could rapidly escalate into a serious crisis, potentially even a war. The operation also revealed that existing bilateral consultative mechanisms for communicating measures that could help defuse tensions during a crisis were largely absent. On a more positive note, some authors have argued that the fact that Indian and Pakistani leaders were able to meet informally to negotiate an end to the standoff was an implicit benefit of SAARC. According to Kishore Dash, this regional body has facilitated the development of "inter-elite reconciliation on many sensitive issues."[19] In his view, "the informal talks between the Indian and Pakistani prime ministers at the second SAARC Summit meeting held in Bangalore in November 1986 led to the diffusion of tensions between the two countries on the issue of India's troop exercise (Operation Brasstacks) on the Indo-Pakistan border."[20]

Although Operation Brasstacks may have been defused on account of the informal institutional context provided by SAARC, it is not clear that such a setting is equipped to handle a more serious threat of war. More importantly, since the foundation of SAARC, the context of the security framework in South Asia has been redrawn on the basis of the underground nuclear tests that India and Pakistan carried out in May 1998, just two years after the signing of the 1996 Comprehensive Test Ban Treaty (CTBT).[21] Although India and Pakistan are not signatories to the CTBT, the 1998 nuclear tests generated a great deal of international pressure to prevent an escalation of the show of force by both countries and to abide by the norms of an international regime on nuclear proliferation. At a regional level, the association has not been able to respond adequately nor has it been able to provide a mechanism for reducing military tensions, largely because military tensions are inherently controversial and are viewed to be a bilateral issue, thus outside of SAARC's remit.

The fact that India and Pakistan, two contiguous military adversaries, are also declared nuclear-capable states has added a new dimension to South Asia's security problems. In this sense, tensions between India and Pakistan cannot be viewed exclusively as a bilateral issue since the repercussions of a nuclear war would have spillover effects in the region. Moreover, the security environment in South Asia has important theoretical implications. In the mainstream neorealist literature on security dilemma theory, the enhancement of a country's security may have the consequence of decreasing the perception of security by another country, which may in turn prompt it to enhance its own defense capabilities as a response. This action, though, may reignite concerns about its own security by the first country, leading to a further enhancement of its own defense capabilities.[22] This cycle of escalation of one's defense capabilities—particularly when the distinction between defensive and offensive military capabilities is ambiguous—can lead to the unintended consequence of making war more likely, even in instances when neither country wishes such an outcome. Under such conditions of an intense security dilemma, William Rose argues that "when security is scarce, arms racing is expected as groups seek military means to protect their interests."[23] The theoretical expectation from such an arms escalation is that "when relative power shifts or is expected to shift, larger and more dangerous windows of vulnerability and opportunity arise. These increase incentives for preventive war."[24]

The decision of India and Pakistan to carry out underground nuclear tests and the fact that China is an implicit military actor in South Asia has altered our traditional understanding of a security balance. Although there has been no explicit war between India and Pakistan since the creation of SAARC, India and Pakistan have engaged in a range of war-like activities, most conspicuously between May and July 1999, in the Kargil district of Indian-administered Kashmir (IAK) and along the actual line of control (LOC) separating India and Pakistan. During the initial stages of this conflict, India accused Pakistan of supporting the incursion of Kashmiri insurgent groups and paramilitary forces from Pakistan-administered Kashmir (PAK) into sections of IAK.[25] The Indian response to these incursions was decisive and led to the capture and withdrawal of these infiltrators from the region. This event, known as the Kargil crisis, has been considered to be extremely important because it highlighted the capacity of Kashmiri insurgents to penetrate the LOC. Indian sensitivities about the penetration of Kashmiri militants into India were tested on 1 October 2001 when Kashmiri insurgents launched an attack on the Jammu and Kashmir legislative assembly in Srinagar. A few weeks later, on 13 December 2001, Kashmiri insurgents launched an assault of the Indian parliament in New Delhi. Although both attacks were foiled by Indian security forces, these incidents precipitated an escalation in the number of Indian and Pakistani troops along the international border and the LOC, reaching nearly one million soldiers from both sides of the border.

The Kargil crisis and the 2001–2 border standoff have also illustrated the potential for a swift escalation of conflict in the region, a particularly worrisome prospect given the fact that both countries are nuclear weapon states. Some authors have argued that, in these circumstances, South Asia is the first explicit instance of a regional nuclear security dilemma.[26] Viewed in this light, overcoming the expected outcomes from a security dilemma and promoting cooperation is one of the biggest challenges for South Asia. However, SAARC has been an exceedingly disappointing actor in attempting to mediate between India and Pakistan. For instance, the summit declaration of the 10th SAARC summit issued in Colombo on 31 July 1998—just a few months after the testing of nuclear weapons by India and Pakistan—made no mention of this dramatic event. The declaration, using language that had appeared in previous summit declarations, alluded to the failure of the nuclear non-proliferation treaty (NNPT) and the CTBT to achieve global nuclear disarmament and non-proliferation.[27] To that effect it underscored its "commitment to the complete elimination of nuclear weapons and the need for promoting nuclear disarmament on a universal basis, under effective international control."[28] Rather than pinpointing the actions by India and Pakistan, the summit leaders "recognised that global non-proliferation goals cannot be achieved in the absence of progress towards nuclear disarmament and in this context called upon all nuclear weapon states, whether party or non-party to the NPT to engage constructively through a transparent and credible process of negotiations at the Conference on Disarmament."[29]

The expectation that SAARC should be a more active driver toward regional cooperation in the security sphere is quite obvious to me, perhaps to the reader as well. Nevertheless, SAARC has shown a great deal of timidity on this issue, even on its own terms. For instance, the clauses in the 10th SAARC summit declaration expressing a commitment to nuclear disarmament on a universal basis, were repeated verbatim in the 11th SAARC summit declaration issued in Kathmandu, Nepal, on 6 January 2002.[30] However, since then, no subsequent SAARC summit declaration has made any mention about the commitment by SAARC member states to support nuclear disarmament and non-proliferation.[31] Instead, the 12th SAARC summit declaration issued in Islamabad, Pakistan, on 6 January 2004 suggested that it envisioned South Asia "to be a peaceful and stable region where each nation is at peace with itself and its neighbours and where conflicts, differences and disputes are addressed through peaceful means and dialogue."[32] To that effect, the 12th SAARC summit declaration encouraged "good neighbourly relations on the basis of the principles of sovereign equality, territorial integrity and national independence, non-use of force, non-intervention and non-interference and peaceful settlement of disputes and recognize[d] the importance of informal political consultations in promoting mutual understanding and reinforcing confidence building processes among Member States."[33]

The view that confidence-building measures (CBMs) could alleviate the intensity of the rivalry between India and Pakistan may appear to be idealistic, perhaps far-fetched.[34] However, this perspective enjoys advocates in policy and academic circles. For instance, in February 1999, the governments of India and Pakistan initiated a policy dialogue, culminating in the signing of a memorandum of understanding between the Indian and Pakistani foreign secretaries whereby both countries agreed to "engage in bilateral consultations on security concepts, and nuclear doctrines, with a view to developing measures for confidence building in the nuclear and conventional fields, aimed at avoidance of conflict."[35] Similarly, Indian prime minister Atal Behari Vajpayee and Pakistani prime minister Nawaz Sharif signed the Lahore Declaration which provided for the development of a bilateral integrated dialogue process and both countries pledged to "take immediate steps for reducing the risk of accidental or unauthorized use of nuclear weapons and discuss concepts and doctrines with a view to elaborating measures for confidence building in the nuclear and conventional fields, aimed at prevention of conflict."[36]

Some recent work on the reduction of rivalry between traditional enemies suggests that lasting peace between adversaries or potential adversaries can be achieved with a series of stabilizing measures which lead to a conflict-free zone.[37] Charles Kupchan's general argument is that in a dyadic conflict scenario where the adversaries have asymmetric levels of strength, the stronger power needs to perform a unilateral act to accommodate the interests of the weaker power. Such an action, argues Kupchan, provides a signal that helps to generate trust and thereby encourages a reciprocal process of restraint and dialogue. Likewise, Sumit Ganguly and Kent Biringer, among others, have argued that stabilizing measures and CBMs could be undertaken to attain a desirable level of crisis stability in South Asia.[38] Although largely developed from a neorealist framework, they offer a helpful range of pragmatic CBMs, including procedural commitments on advance notification of troop movements and the launch of nuclear-capable missiles as well as the monitoring and inspection options of nuclear facilities. Ganguly and Biringer, though, argue that the effectiveness of CBMs in South Asia is curtailed by the mutually reinforcing suspicions between Indian and Pakistani leaders. They suggest (and implicitly reject as highly unlikely) the view that if an external power—like China or the United States—could guarantee the security of one or both parties, then the mutual doubts and suspicions might abate. However, in the absence of an external power that can guarantee security, then perhaps another alternative should be considered. SAARC, for instance, is a permanent institutionalized mechanism that could oversee the implementation of certain CBMs in the region.

Although this regional body may not have the technical capability to undertake some forms of military CBMs, such as standard verification measures (e.g., aerial inspections, ground-based sensory systems), it is possible to adapt some existing SAARC procedures with a view to the implementation of more concrete CBMs. For instance, one of the pillars of the composite dialogue between India and Pakistan that followed the 1999 Lahore Declaration was the proposal for a series of friendly, people-to-people exchanges between India and Pakistan, notably through the re-establishment of a bus service linking Srinagar and Muzaffarabad (the capitals of IAK and PAK, respectively).[39] One of the key obstacles to the successful operation of the bus service has been the complexity of the visa regime governing the transit of individuals from this region. However, SAARC has enacted a visa exemption scheme that could easily be applied to this particular CBM. Similarly, the potentially thorny issue of carrying out a joint survey of the barrage pillars along the Sir Creek estuary (along the India-Pakistan border) could easily be undertaken by a team of geologists under the aegis of SAARC.

SAARC's potential support for CBMs in the region need not be limited to those stemming from the traditional animosity between India and Pakistan. Nor should one conceive of this regional body as being an institution that would supplant other national forms of surveillance. However, SAARC has developed a reputation for neutrality that could easily be transformed for more effective purposes. For instance, SAARC could—once again—learn from the AU by developing a small, regional peace-keeping force. In an era when the UN has become overwhelmed by increasing peace-keeping demands, the development of a SAARC-based equivalent institution could be quite beneficial to a region that is prone to devastating natural catastrophes. The 2001 earthquake in Gujarat, the 2004 Indian Ocean tsunami, the 2005 earthquake in Kashmir, the 2007 mudslides in Bangladesh, and the 2010 floods in Pakistan, are just some of the major natural disasters that have severely affected the region in recent years. In many such instances, the ineffective delivery of humanitarian assistance at the first instance was a substantial contributor to a higher civilian death toll. At present, SAARC has three existing regional centers devoted to natural disasters (i.e., the SAARC Meteorological Research Center, the SAARC Disaster Management Center, and the SAARC Coastal Zone Management Center). However, they merely exist as information-gathering centers. The development of a SAARC peace-keeping force with the potential for rapid deployment to regional areas affected by natural disasters could be an operational asset to the delivery of humanitarian assistance and the prevention of post-disaster epidemics. Peace-keeping forces and rapid response teams from South Asia are already operational in other parts of the world, so the idea of developing a SAARC-sponsored team should not be considered intractable. Ultimately, as one observer has noted, "given the political realities of the day, SAARC cannot pretend to be a conflict-resolving mechanism through misplaced cooperation, but only a cooperation-promoting device in feasible areas."[40]

## Challenges to economic cooperation

Students of the effectiveness of CBMs in South Asia have also pointed to other types of non-military CBMs, notably in the form of economic CBMs. The implicit assumption behind the proposal for economic CBMs is that nations that trade with each other have a diminished incentive to wage war against each other. For instance, in proposing economic CBMs between India and Pakistan in light of the pattern of trade between both countries, a pre-eminent Pakistani economist, Akbar Zaidi, has argued that "there is no economic rationale and justification for either of the two countries not to trade with each other, especially in an era of globalisation and liberalisation."[41]

There are, however, some limitations to the expectation that trade itself may be an adequate foil to interregional conflict. In an insightful critique of regional cooperation in South Asia, Syedur Rahman observed that there were two factors limiting cooperation in the region. First, the delinking of the colonially established economies of India and Pakistan. Second, the similarity of the trading patterns of the core regional actors.[42] Other scholars, including myself, have provided empirical support to the view that South Asian economies trade little with each other on account of the incongruent nature of their principal manufactured exports, rather than on the basis of unfriendly political relations.[43] Accordingly, in this book, particularly in Chapter 3, I have also highlighted important developments in economic integration, both in terms of low volume and uneven growth in regional exports as a proportion of total exports.

Nevertheless, we should pay special attention to other forms of interregional trade that may provide an avenue for greater regional collaboration. As students of South Asia are aware, the region is unique compared to other low-income economies insofar as services account for a substantial proportion of GDP. Table 5.1, for instance, shows that services as a proportion of GDP are very high in the Maldives (exceeding 76 percent in 2008) and they amount to more than half of overall GDP in Bangladesh, India, Pakistan, and Sri Lanka.[44]

The data in Table 5.1 provide evidence that South Asian economies are heavily reliant on services. Accordingly, one may assume that an increase in intraregional trade in services would have beneficial spillover effects on regional GDP. As discussed in Chapter 3, though, until recently SAARC has not been an advocate of increased trade in services. Rather than focusing on traditional, state-based approaches to increase regional trade, through the mechanism of free trade area arrangements, SAARC could redirect its efforts to removing non-tariff-based barriers to entry, particularly in the services sector.

Moreover, the transportation of goods within SAARC member states has been hampered by poor physical infrastructure. For instance, according to one estimate, in the absence of direct rail container links between India and Bangladesh, it takes 45 days to transport a train container from Delhi to Dhaka by road.[45] The road networks linking the principal sectoral trading partners in South Asia (e.g., Nepal and India, Bangladesh and India) are inoperable on a grand scale, and in some cases are completely inaccessible due to national security concerns. Even with the presence of adequate infrastructure links, the existing visa regime adopted by all South Asian countries is inimical to sustainable trade or investment relationships.[46] At present, the only policy innovation proposed by SAARC has been a visa exemption scheme, mostly relating to the simplification of visa procedures and requirements. However, there is only a limited range of individuals (e.g., parliamentarians, government ministers, judges of the Supreme Court, or SAARC Secretariat officials) who are able to take advantage of the SAARC visa exemption scheme.

*Table 5.1* Services as a proportion of GDP among South Asian countries, 2008

| *Country* | *Percentage* |
|---|---|
| Afghanistan | 42.1 |
| Bangladesh | 52.5 |
| Bhutan | 35.2 |
| India | 53.7 |
| Maldives | 76.1 |
| Nepal | 49.6 |
| Pakistan | 52.7 |
| Sri Lanka | 57.3 |

Source: World Bank, World Development Indicators.

Moreover, ancillary activities relating to trade, such as banking and telecommunications, need greater attention. There is no doubt that security concerns relating to transnational terrorism have also hindered the development of a South Asian-based civil aviation regime.

In trying to evaluate what level of economic integration has taken place in South Asia and what role SAARC may have played in enhancing such economic integration, it may be useful to understand different levels of economic integration. Bela Balassa's classic typology of economic integration incorporates five developmental stages: a free trade area; a customs union; a common market; an economic union; and total economic integration.[47] According to Balassa's typology, attached to each stage of this economic integration process there is a corresponding removal of some key feature of discrimination among economic units, ranging from the removal of tariffs or quotas, common external tariffs, free flow of factors, harmonization of economic policies, and ultimately the unification of policies and political institutions. In this sense, SAARC has facilitated the creation of a free trade area through the SAPTA.

Could South Asia, with SAARC as a mediating institutional vehicle, increase its level of economic integration while bypassing political integration? Such an outcome is unlikely on two fronts. First, the theoretical expectation would be that cooperation resulting from the expected gains from trade would weaken if actual gains are unevenly distributed. Second, enhanced economic integration, as suggested earlier, would necessitate the harmonization of economic policies and, ultimately, the convergence of policies with political institutions. Given the current structural configuration of policy-making in SAARC—with the constraint of unanimity among its member states—and the self-imposed demand that no controversial subject matters can be broached in SAARC summits, it would be far-fetched to imagine that there could be supranationality of decisions on important economic matters. In an insightful analysis of the pattern of regional cooperation in South Asia, Shrikant Paranjpe argues that SAARC "appears to have adopted the Nordic model of regional co-operation; that is, an avoidance of the 'constitutional' approach, an understanding that the national structure would remain the unalterable political basis for co-operation that would be directed to areas of relatively 'low' political content, and the exclusion of areas of 'high' political content (such as national security) from regional co-operation."[48]

## Challenges to social and developmental integration

I have also shown that there has been some increase in social integration, primarily through trade in goods and services. Other authors have suggested that there has been a gradual increase in regional connectivity, namely in terms of aggregate growth in mass and elite-level transactions, such as the number of intraregional air passengers, tourists, student and scholarly exchanges, energy, and mail.[49] Although many of the issues addressed by the SAARC regional centers could contribute to an increase in social integration, compared to the growth of economic integration, the actual evidence for an increase in social integration remains quite modest.

Social and developmental integration is not possible, at present, due to a number of structural economic features of South Asia. As outlined throughout this book, there are differences in population size, stages of economic development, natural resource endowment, and degree of industrialization. Writing at the time of the creation of SAARC, some authors idealistically believed that, despite these disparities, "the prospects for regional cooperation in South Asia are great in so far as the solution to the common problems is concerned."[50] Another author, optimistic about the prospects for regional collaboration, wrote about South Asia as being "much more of a single ecosystem."[51] However, the basic premise from that perspective is that the prospects for the success of regional cooperation could not be guaranteed "unless it ensures a balanced inter-dependence among the partners in terms of equitable sharing of gains and losses. Regional cooperation is not only a question of mutuality of benefits but also social justice."[52]

In contrast, one could argue that the reason that regional integration under a SAARC banner has not worked is due to the association's excessive concern for equity. Instead, the future focus of the association should be on promoting political integration among the member states of SAARC, taking into account that different actors will have asymmetrical levels of resource endowments and power. In that manner, then, differences in the allocation of benefits could be negotiated politically, rather than administratively. At present, political integration in South Asia is extremely limited, principally to a basic level of bureaucratic convergence in the operation and management of the SAARC Secretariat.

In Chapter 4 we learnt that one of the most important obstacles to the effectiveness of SAARC initiatives is the impact of domestic legislation at the implementation stage. Abul Ahsan, SAARC's first secretary general, commented that the transformation of SAARC "from being a framework for regular get-togethers, exchange of information and experiences to an effective instrument for collective action will take time to evolve."[53] In Ahsan's view, the speed at which this transformation takes place "will first of all depend upon the ability of the member states to harmonize and accommodate their differing interests and attitudes on certain basic political security and foreign policy issues."[54] One possible solution for greater political integration of SAARC member states would be the creation of a SAARC Parliament, akin to the European Parliament or the AU's Pan-African Parliament.[55] However, given the disparity in political regimes in South Asia (with its history of extended authoritarian rule and unstable democracies) any possibility that a SAARC Parliament would be more effective than the current institutional structures is vitiated.

In that sense, one of the most critical ingredients to the success of a regional institution lies in its capacity to promote political integration. According to Joseph Nye, there are four types of political integration: institutional (both in terms of bureaucratic and jurisdictional convergence); policy; attitudinal; and security community.[56] It is hard to foresee how SAARC, as a mechanism of regional integration in South Asia will be able to transcend the lack of political integration. However, one can remain optimistic on the basis of past experience elsewhere. Using an example from East Africa, for instance, Nye showed that growth in economic integration need not correspond to growing levels of political integration. Nye also postulated that transactions of social integration may be a "misleading indicator of political integration."[57] Based on the experience of 20 years since the establishment of SAARC, it is clear that South Asia's economic integration has outpaced social and political integration.

Analysts who have argued for greater monetary cooperation in South Asia are keenly aware that the experience in other countries shows "the critical importance of political commitment among members to ensure the success of this process."[58] There is some evidence that there has been a modest increase in the bureaucratic integration, based on the budgetary allocation by SAARC member states to the operational side of the association. However, in terms of jurisdictional convergence (using Nye's categories), namely supranationality of decisions, legal scope, and the expansion of jurisdiction, there is little evidence that there has been much political integration in South Asia.

Building on these assumptions, then, it is reasonable to conclude that many regional institutions like SAARC reach a plateau in terms of performance. Although economic integration has moved fastest, it would be unable to progress beyond the creation of a common market without a corresponding increase in political integration. In this sense, SAARC has enabled greater *regionalization,* namely in the form of an increased regional concentration of economic flows. As Albert Fishlow and Stephen Haggard argue, though, regionalization is distinct from *regionalism*, a process that they imbue with specific *political* characteristics. They frame the concept of regionalization as the outcome of a political process that reaches specific economic policy decisions.[59] Viewed in this way, SAARC has not achieved a sufficient level of institutionalization to act a vehicle for regionalism.

As SAARC celebrate its 25th anniversary, it is important to establish that the institution must be transformed to develop into an effective tool of regional collaboration. In one of the initial assessments of the prospects for SAARC, Sumit Ganguly correctly predicted that "it is unlikely that any dramatic cooperative ventures will be launched in the foreseeable future. The seven nations will continue to meet, they will continue to bicker and they will, hopefully, find some small common grounds to achieve a modicum of cooperation."[60]

To conclude, I have outlined some future challenges facing the association, but most importantly offered some concrete suggestions for overcoming these obstacles. The structural bias in SAARC has been to embrace a diffuse range of ineffective initiatives. In some respects, SAARC needs to learn lessons from its own successes and failures over the years. However, it is also important for SAARC to be less insular in its outlook and to learn from other similar institutions. To that effect, one's attention may be drawn towards the European Community or ASEAN. However, based on similarities in developmental and regional complexity, SAARC could learn most from the AU. The institutional development from the OAU to the AU is a lesson on how to add contemporary relevance to what many considered to be a moribund and ineffective institution. If SAARC is to avoid the criticism of being irrelevant, it must transform itself in terms of institutional design and operational focus.

# Notes

## Foreword

1 The descriptor of emerging powers has never sat well with India, China and Brazil. See Oliver Turner, "China's Recovery: Why the Writing Was Always on the Wall,"*The Political Quarterly* 80, no. 1 (2009): 111–18.
2 Goldman Sachs' 2003 designation of Brazil, Russia, India, and China as the BRICs—that is, those economies that were most likely to figure in the list of the top six by 2050—has since given way to a focus on only Brazil, India, and China. The loss of faith among international financiers in Russia's core economic model is the explanation.
3 Another Goldman Sachs construction, this time referring to Bangladesh, Egypt, Indonesia, Iran, Mexico, Nigeria, Pakistan, the Philippines, South Korea, Turkey, and Vietnam as the next most likely leading economies in 2050.
4 The interest the BICs and Next 11 has generated is often not so much about these countries but more about what the West can do to stem their challenge.
5 Lawrence Sáez, *Federalism without a Center: The Impact of Political Reform and Economic Liberalization on India's Federal System* (New Delhi, India: Sage Publications, 2002); and *Banking Reform in India and China* (New York: Palgrave Macmillan, 2004); and Katherine Adeney and Lawrence Sáez, eds., *Coalition Politics and Hindu Nationalism* (London: Routledge, 2005).
6 On Africa: Ian Taylor, *The Forum on China-Africa Cooperation* (2011); Kwame Akonor, *African Economic Institutions* (2010); and Samuel M. Makinda and F. Wafula Okumu, *The African Union* (2008). On Europe: Clive Archer, *The European Union* (2008); and David J. Galbreath, *The Organization for Security and Co-operation in Europe* (2007). On the Americas: Monica Herz, *The Organization of American States* (2011).

## Introduction

1 For illustrative examples, see Kant Bhargava and Ross Masood Husain, *SAARC and European Union* (New Delhi, India: Har-Anand Publications, 1994); Kant Bhargava, *EU-SAARC: Comparisons and Prospects of Cooperation*, ZEI Discussion Paper C15 (1998); Sonu Trivedi, *Regional Economic Cooperation and Integration: COMESA, EU, SAARC* (New Delhi: New Century Publishers, 2005); Joseph Francois, Pradumna Rana, Ganeshan Wignaraja, eds., *National Strategies for Regional Integration: South and East*

*Asian Case Studies* (London: Anthem Press and Asian Development Bank, 2009); Bangladesh Institute of International and Strategic Studies, *ASEAN Experiences of Regional and Inter-Regional Cooperation: Relevance for SAARC* (Dhaka: Bangladesh Institute of International and Strategic Studies, 1988); Bharati Chhibber, *Regional Security and Regional Cooperation: A Comparative Study of ASEAN and SAARC* (New Delhi, India: New Century Publications, 2004); Bhabani Sen Gupta, *SAARC-ASEAN: Prospects and Problems of Inter-Regional Cooperation* (New Delhi: South Asian Publishers, 1988); and Kripa Sridharan, *Regional Organizations and Conflict Management: Comparing ASEAN and SAARC*, Working Paper 2, no. 3 (London: Crisis States Research Center, 2008).

2 A notable exception to this dearth of comparative institutional work is Sonu Trivedi, "SAARC-COMESA: Exploring South–South Co-operation," *Journal of Developing Studies* 22, no. 1 (2006): 57–73.

3 O. P. Goel, *India and SAARC Engagements* (New Delhi, India: Isha Books, 2004).

4 Dhirendra Dwivedi, *SAARC: Problems and Prospects* (New Delhi, India: Adhyayan Publishers, 2008).

5 Data on share of regional GDP have been calculated by me based on data from the World Bank, *World Development Indicators* (Washington, DC: World Bank Group, 2010).

6 Data on military force capabilities calculated by me. International Institute for Strategic Studies, *The Military Balance 2010* (London: IISS, 2010), 357–70.

7 Data on military expenditures have been calculated by me. Stockholm International Peace Research Institute, *SIPRI Yearbook 2010* (Stockholm, Sweden: SIPRI, 2010).

8 Goel, *India and SAARC Engagements*. Unfortunately, many analysts of SAARC have adopted a similar approach. For instance, Farhat Eshas' *SAARC: Relevance in the New World Order* (New Delhi: Reference Press, 2003), also frames the evaluation of SAARC from the perspective of India. One of the chapters in this book explicitly devotes one chapter to "the Major Player (India)." In my view, these perspectives are not likely to build a more holistic understanding of regional institutions.

9 Kishore Dash, *Regionalism in South Asia: Negotiating Cooperation, Institutional Structures* (London: Routledge, 2008).

10 Ranjan Modi, *SAARC: Regional and Global Perspectives* (Jaipur, India: Mangal Deep Publications, 2004).

11 Frank Schimmelfennig and Ulrich Sedelmeier, "Theorizing EU Enlargement: Research Focus, Hypotheses, and the State of Research," *Journal of European Public Policy* 9, no. 4 (2002): 503.

12 The literature on European Union enlargement is far too extensive to summarize here. For illustrative examples of the literature on the expected theoretical difficulties of EU enlargement, see Richard Baldwin, "The Eastern Enlargement of the European Union," *European Economic Review* 39, no. 3–4 (1995): 474–81; Andrew Moravcsik, "Reassessing Legitimacy in the European Union," *Journal of Common Market Studies* 40, no. 4 (2002): 603–24; and Neill Nugent, ed., *European Union Enlargement* (New York: Palgrave Macmillan, 2004).

13 Jeffrey Checkel, "Norms, Institutions, and National Identity in Contemporary Europe," *International Studies Quarterly* 43, no. 1 (1999): 108.

14 Jeffrey Legro, "Which Norms Matter? Revisiting the 'Failure' of Internationalism," *International Organization* 51, no. 1 (1997): 36.
15 Barry Buzan, Ole Wæver, and Jaap de Wide, *Security: A New Framework for Analysis* (Boulder, Col.: Lynne Rienner, 1998).
16 Mely Caballero-Anthony, "Understanding the Dynamics of Securitizing Non-Traditional Security," in *Understanding Non-Traditional Security in Asia: Dilemmas in Securitization,* eds. Mely Caballero-Anthony, Ralf Emmers, and Amitav Acharya (London: Ashgate, 2006), 1–12; Amitav Acharya, "Securitizing in Asia: Formative and Normative Implications," in *Understanding Non-Traditional Security in Asia: Dilemmas in Securitization*, eds. Mely Caballero-Anthony, Ralf Emmers, and Amitav Acharya, 247–50; Claire Wilkinson, "The Copenhagen School on Tour in Kyrgyzstan: Is Securitization Theory Useable Outside Europe?," *Security Dialogue* 38, no. 1 (2007): 1–22; and Monika Barthwal-Datta, "Securitising Threats Without the State: A Case Study of Misgovernance as a Security Threat in Bangladesh," *Review of International Studies* 35, no. 2 (2009): 277–300.
17 D. K. Ghosh, *New Frontiers: Pathways for SAARC* (New Delhi, India: Sunrise Publications, 2004).
18 Anil Bhuimali and Chandan Mukhopadhyay, *Economic Issues in SAARC Context* (Delhi, India: Abhijeet Publications, 2008).
19 For instance, the opening chapter in this edited volume is on "efficient and minimum mean squared ARIMA forecast for GDP in the economy of India by the Box-Jenkins (BJ) methodology."
20 See, for instance, Samuel Makinda and Wafula Okumu, *The African Union: Challenges of Globalization, Security, and Governance* (London: Routledge, 2008).

**1 SAARC membership and structure**

1 Andrew Hurrell, "Explaining the Resurgence of Regionalism in World Politics," *Review of International Studies* 21, no. 4 (1995): 335.
2 An excellent overview of the apparent difficulties that would hinder SAARC from achieving regional cooperation can be found in Lok Raj Baral, "SARC, But Not 'SHARK': South Asian Regional Cooperation in Perspective," *Pacific Affairs* 58, no. 3 (1985): 411–26.
3 See, for instance, Sinderpal Singh, "Framing 'South Asia': Whose Imagined Region?" *Institute of Defense and Strategic Studies Working Paper*, no. 9 (Singapore: IDSS, 2001): 8.
4 J. S. Furnivall, "South Asia in the World Today," in *South Asia in the World Today*, ed. Phillips Talbot (Chicago: Chicago University Press, 1950), 3.
5 Phillips Talbot, "Preface," in *South Asia in the World Today*, ed. Talbot, vi.
6 See, for instance, Theodore Morgan, "The Underdeveloped Area Expert: South Asia Model," *Economic Development and Cultural Change* 2, no. 1 (1953): 27–31; Ali Tayyeb, "Geo-Economic Trends in South Asia," *The Canadian Journal of Economics and Political Science / Revue Canadienne d'Economique et de Science Politique* 18, no. 3 (1952): 358–64; and Charles Wolf, Jr., "Some Reflections on the Status of Economic Development in South and Southeast Asia: Report of a Trip," *Economic Development and Cultural Change* 2, no. 3 (1954): 198–208.

7 Sumit Ganguly, "The Prospects for SAARC," in *Dilemmas of National Security and Cooperation in India and Pakistan*, ed. Hafeez Malik (New York: St. Martin's Press, 1993), 276; Muhammad Jamshed Iqbal, "SAARC: Origin, Growth, Potential and Achievements," *Pakistan Journal of History & Culture* 27, no. 2 (2006): 131; Sisir Gupta, *India and Regional Integration in Asia* (Bombay, India: Asia Publishing House, 1964), 36 and 47; and Michael Haas, *The Asian Way to Peace* (New York: Praeger, 1989), 276.

8 Dipankar Banerjee, "Towards Comprehensive and Cooperative Security in South Asia," *South Asian Survey* 6, no. 2 (1999): 314; Kanti Bajpai and Stephen Cohen, "Co-operative Security and South Asian Insecurity," in *Global Engagement: Co-operation and Security in the 21st Century*, ed. Jane Nolan (Washington, DC: The Brookings Institution, 1994), 447–80. The Colombo Powers Conference was attended by representatives from Burma, Ceylon, India, Indonesia, and Pakistan.

9 The original members of the Colombo Plan included Australia, Britain, Canada, Ceylon, India, New Zealand, and Pakistan.

10 For further reference, see Timothy Shaw, *Commonwealth: Inter- and Non-State Contributions to Global Governance* (London: Routledge, 2008).

11 "Ties with Nepal," *Bangladesh Times*, 21 December 1977.

12 "India and Bangladesh Want Ties Developed Further," *The Statesman*, 24 December 1977.

13 "Non-interference Has Guided Delhi, Dacca Ties," *Hindustan Times*, 20 December 1977.

14 "Basis of Understanding," *Bangladesh Times*, 23 December 1977.

15 "Mission of Peace," *Bangladesh Times*, 25 December 1977.

16 "President Zia's Tour of the Subcontinent," *Bangladesh Observer*, 25 December 1977.

17 "Visits Positively Successful," *Bangladesh Times*, 14 December 1977.

18 Major General Rahman became president of Bangladesh on 21 April 1977, just a few months before his historic December 1977 tour of South Asian countries. After his accession to power, though, President Rahman's government was challenged by a number of military mutinies. Eventually, he was able to consolidate his hold on power and founded a new political party, the Bangladesh Nationalist Party, which has become one of the two major political parties in the country. Nevertheless, the cycle of political instability in Bangladesh was not complete as President Rahman was himself killed in a failed *coup d'état* on 30 May 1981.

19 "Quest for Credibility," *The Statesman*, 17 December 1977.

20 Kishore Dash, "The Political Economy of Regional Cooperation in South Asia," *Pacific Affairs* 69, no. 2 (1996): 186.

21 The RCD was a precursor to the Economic Cooperation Organization (ECO). Further details about the foundation of the RCD can be found in Behçet Kemal Yeşilbursa, "The Formation of RCD: Regional Cooperation for Development," *Middle Eastern Studies* 45, no. 4 (July 2009): 637–60.

22 Syed Muazzam Ali, "Remembering Kibria: A Legend of Our Time," *Dhaka Courier*, 2 February 2010. Kibria was killed in 2005 in a grenade attack that took place on the occasion of the 13th SAARC summit held in Dhaka, Bangladesh.

23 Ministry of Foreign Affairs, Government of Bangladesh, *Paper on the Proposal for a Regional Cooperation in South Asia* (Dhaka, Bangladesh: Ministry of

Foreign Affairs, 1980). Also see, "A Paper on the Proposal for Regional Cooperation in South Asia," *From SARC to SAARC: Milestones in the Evolution of Regional Cooperation in South Asia (1980–1988), Volume I* (Kathmandu: SAARC Secretariat, 1988), 1–8. A reproduction of this document is also available in Abul Ahsan, *SAARC: A Perspective* (Dhaka, Bangladesh: University Press Limited, 1992), 27–40.

24 Faruq Choudhury, "Evolution of SAARC," *Bangladesh Observer*, 7 December 1985.

25 "India Goes to Colombo Meet with Caution," *Hindustan Times*, 20 April 1981.

26 Umashanker Phadnis, "Colombo Marks a Modest Start," *Hindustan Times*, 25 April 1981.

27 Imtiaz Bokhari, "South Asian Regional Cooperation: Progress, Problems, Potential, and Prospects," *Asian Survey* 25, no. 4 (1985): 375. Bokhari argues that India and Pakistan were opposed to the creation of a formal institutional arrangement.

28 Bokhari, "South Asian Regional Cooperation: Progress, Problems, Potential, and Prospects," 379.

29 Declaration of South Asian Regional Cooperation issued in New Delhi, 2 August 1983. *From SARC to SAARC: Milestones in the Evolution of Regional Cooperation in South Asia (1980–1988), Volume I* (Kathmandu, Nepal: SAARC Secretariat, 1988): 58–60.

30 The full text of the declaration can be found in "7 Asian Nations Resolve to Step Up Co-Operation," *Hindustan Times*, 3 August 1983, 1. Also see "Foreign Ministers Sign Joint Plan of Action," *The Statesman*, 3 August 1983.

31 Emanual Nahar, *SAARC: Problems and Prospects* (New Delhi, India: Sehgal Publishers, 1991), 21.

32 A detailed descriptive account of the development surrounding the first SAARC summit can be found in Pramod Kumar Mishra, *Dhaka Summit and SAARC: A Broad Overview* (Calcutta, India: Netaji Institute for Asian Studies, 1986).

33 Since the time of his first election, President Gayoom has been the longest serving president of the Maldives.

34 Ahmed Fazl, "SARC Will Reverse Colonial Process," *Bangladesh Times*, 4 December 1985.

35 Sudhin Day, "Dhaka Summit Sets Up S. Asian Panel," *The Statesman*, 9 December 1985.

36 Hussain Muhammed Ershad, "Seven Perfumed Prospects," *Bangladesh Observer*, 7 December 1985. At the end of his concluding speech at the first SAARC summit, President Ershad read out another poem, entitled "In Warm Animation," in which he envisioned that "in glittering sunshine the seven sovereign flags flutter happily in the new Zone of Hope."

37 "Zia's Dilemma in Dhaka," *Hindustan Times*, 8 December 1985.

38 N. C. Menon, "Problems and Promise of SAARC," *Hindustan Times*, 11 December 1985.

39 SAARC Charter, Preamble.

40 SAARC Charter, Article 1.

41 SAARC Charter, Article 2.

42 SAARC Charter, Article 10.1.

43 SAARC Charter, Article 10.2. These two general provisions, together with the SAARC objectives and principles found in Article 1 and 2 of the SAARC

Charter, were identical to the general provisions adopted at the Declaration on South Asian Regional Cooperation during the first meeting of South Asian foreign ministers on 1–2 August 1983.

44 SAARC Charter, Article 3.
45 SAARC Charter, Article 4.1.
46 SAARC Charter, Article 5.1.
47 SAARC Charter, Article 5.2.
48 SAARC Charter, Article 5.3.
49 SAARC Charter, Article 6.1.
50 SAARC Charter, Article 6.3.
51 SAARC Charter, Article 6.3.
52 SAARC Charter, Article 7.
53 SAARC Charter, Article 8.
54 "Need for Secretariat Stressed," *Bangladesh Observer*, 6 December 1985, 1.
55 "SARC is Born," *Bangladesh Observer*, 8 December 1985.
56 *Memorandum of Understanding on the Establishment of the Secretariat* (Kathmandu, Nepal: SAARC Secretariat, 1987). The document was signed on 17 November 1986 in Bangalore, India.
57 Quoted in Lok Raj Baral, "Nepal in 1987: Politics Without Power," *Asian Survey* 28, no. 2 (February 1988): 178.
58 Satish Misra, "SAARC in Review," *Link*, January 1987, 60.
59 Abul Ahsan, *SAARC: A Perspective* (Dhaka, Bangladesh: University Press Ltd, 1992), 21.
60 9th SAARC summit declaration, issued on 14 May 1997 in Malé, Maldives.
61 O. P. Shah, "Institutional Capacity Building and Expansion of SAARC," *BIISS Journal* 25, no. 4 (October 2004): 350.
62 SAARC Charter, Article 9.1.
63 SAARC Charter, Article 9.2.
64 SAARC Charter, Article 9.3.
65 Memorandum of Understanding on the Establishment of the Secretariat, Article 8.3.
66 Memorandum of Understanding on the Establishment of the Secretariat, Article 6.1.
67 Memorandum of Understanding on the Establishment of the Secretariat, Article 6.2.
68 Memorandum of Understanding on the Establishment of the Secretariat, Article 6.3.
69 Ahsan, *SAARC: A Perspective*, 21.
70 Ahsan, *SAARC: A Perspective*, 21.
71 Shah, "Institutional Capacity Building and Expansion of SAARC," 351.
72 During interviews with me, it was noted that some issues bypass Working Divisions altogether and are presented directly to the Standing Committee for its approval. However, I did not obtain clarification on why some issues bypass preliminary discussion at Working Division level or who decides which issues should be brought up before the Standing Committee.
73 The specific SAARC conventions and agreements will be discussed in separate sections of this book.
74 *SAARC Vision Beyond the Year 2000: Report of the SAARC Group of Eminent Persons Established by the Ninth SAARC Summit* (New Delhi, India: Shipra Publications, 1999), xxvi.

## 2 The enlargement of SAARC

1 John Ruggie, ed., *Multilateralism Matters: The Theory and Praxis of an Institutional Form* (New York: Columbia University Press, 1993), 14.

2 See Ian Taylor, *United Nations Conference on Trade and Development* (London: Routledge, 2007), and Barry Buzan, "Negotiating by Consensus: Developments in Technique at the United Nations Conference on the Law of the Sea," *American Journal of International Law* 75, no. 2 (1981): 324–48.

3 Building upon a Russian-led Collective Security Treaty Organization (CSTO), China has successfully steered the SCO to suit its strategic interests. The result of a 1996 multilateral treaty with precise military objectives, the Treaty on Deepening Military Trust in Border Regions, the SCO initially defined its primary objectives in the form of common security concerns in Central Asia.

4 Since the signing of the SCO Charter in 2002, the SCO has also highlighted the importance of developing a regional anti-terrorism structure and later promoted the idea of increasing economic cooperation between the SCO member states through a free trade area in Central Asia. The SCO has gradually adopted the position that multilateral collaboration in trade, energy science, and technology should be adopted by the member states, including proposals for a harmonization of tax rates to improve trade. For some perspectives on this shift, see Ariel Cohen, "The Dragon Looks West: China and the Shanghai Cooperation Organization," Heritage Lectures, No. 961 (Washington, DC: Heritage Foundation, 2006); and Christopher Brown, "China's Central Asian Reach – The Shanghai Cooperation Organization and the China Russia Bi-Lateral Relationship." Testimony before the Subcommittee on Oversight and Investigations, House International Relations Committee. US House of Representatives, 14 December 2005.

5 See, for instance, Clive Archer, *The European Union* (London: Routledge, 2008), and Julian Lindley-French, *The North Atlantic Treaty Organization: The Enduring Alliance* (London: Routledge, 2007).

6 See, for instance, O. P. Goel, *India and SAARC Engagements* (New Delhi, India: Isha Books, 2004), Farhat Eshas, *SAARC: Relevance in the New World Order* (New Delhi, India: Reference Press, 2003).

7 Prior to the creation of SAARC, a special issue of the prestigious journal, *Asian Survey*, offered a country-to-country perspective on the emerging regional architecture. See "SARC: Four Views and a Comparative Perspective (special issue)," *Asian Survey* 25, no. 4 (April 1985). Other notable examples of country-to-country perspectives on SAARC include Lok Raj Baral, *The Politics of Balanced Interdependence* (New Delhi, India: Sterling Publishers, 1988); Iftekharuzzaman and Imtiaz Ahmed, *Bangladesh and SAARC: Issues, Perspectives, and Outlook* (Dhaka, Bangladesh: Academic Publishers, 1992); and Rajesh Kharat, *Bhutan in SAARC: Role of a Small State in a Regional Alliance* (New Delhi, India: South Asian Publishers, 1999).

8 Ted Hopf, "The Promise of Constructivism in International Relations Theory," *International Security* 23, no. 1 (1998): 176.

9 Hopf, "The Promise of Constructivism in International Relations Theory," 175.

10 Hopf, "The Promise of Constructivism in International Relations Theory," 193.

11 Alexander Wendt, "Anarchy is What States Make of It: The Social Construction of Power Politics," *International Organization* 46, no. 2 (Spring 1992): 398.

12 Frank Schimmelfennig and Ulrich Sedelmeier, "Theorizing EU Enlargement: Research Focus, Hypotheses, and the State of Research," *Journal of European Public Policy* 9, no. 4 (2002): 503.
13 Schimmelfennig and Sedelmeier, "Theorizing EU Enlargement: Research Focus, Hypotheses, and the State of Research," 503.
14 Alexander Wendt, *Social Theory of International Politics* (Cambridge: Cambridge University Press, 1999), 365.
15 Chris Ogden has made important inroads in the application of constructivist theoretical frameworks to our understanding of Indian foreign policy. See, for instance, Chris Ogden, "Norms, Indian Foreign Policy and 1998–2004 National Democratic Alliance," *The Round Table* 99, no. 408 (2010): 303–15; and Chris Ogden, "Post-Colonial, Pre-BJP: The Normative Parameters of India's Security Identity, 1947–98," *Asian Journal of Political Science* 17, no. 2 (2009): 215–37.
16 O.P. Shah, "Institutional Capacity Building and Expansion of SAARC," *BIISS Journal* 25, no. 4 (2004): 358.
17 Shah, "Institutional Capacity Building and Expansion of SAARC," 358.
18 Shamina Nasreen, "Inclusion of Afghanistan in SAARC: From Reluctance to Sudden Rush," *The Daily Star*, 18 February 2010.
19 Nasreen, "Inclusion of Afghanistan in SAARC: From Reluctance to Sudden Rush."
20 "Afghanistan's Entry Okayed," *Times of India*, 14 November 2005.
21 "Afghanistan to be New Member," *The Daily Star*, 14 November 2005.
22 For instance, one of the most serious incidents of communal violence in contemporary India emerged on the basis of conflicting claims made about the location of the Babri Masjid, a mosque that was built by Babur in the town of Ayodhya, India.
23 In 1829, Alexander von Humboldt conducted a research expedition at the invitation by Tsar Nicholas I. Based on the geographic and physical characteristics of the region he explored, he termed the highland region between the Altai mountains, the Himalaya mountains, the greater Hinggan and the Turan Depression as Central-Asien. Humboldt's major work on this area was published in 1844. See Alexander von Humboldt, *Central-Asien: Untersuchungen über die Gebirgsketten und die vergleichende Klimatologie*, 2 volumes (Berlin: Klemann, 1844). However, earlier references to Central-Asien can be found in Humboldt's personal travel narratives. See, for instance, Alexander von Humboldt and Aimé Bonpland, *Personal Narrative of Travels to the Equinoctial Regions of the New Continent during the Years 1799–1804* (Volume 5). Available at: http://www.avhumboldt.net. See also http://eeo.uni-klu.ac.at/index.php/Zentralasien.
24 See Friedrich von Hellwald, *Centralasien: Landschaften und Völker in Kaschgar, Turkestan, Kaschmir und Tibet* (Leipzig, Germany: Spamer, 1875).
25 Statement by his Excellency Hamid Karzai, President of the Islamic Republic of Afghanistan, at the 14th summit of the South Asian Association for Regional Cooperation, 3–4 April 2007, Delhi, India. Available at: www.saarc-sec.org/data/summit14/afgprez.doc.
26 Statement by his Excellency Hamid Karzai, President of the Islamic Republic of Afghanistan, at the 14th summit of the South Asian Association for Regional Cooperation, 3–4 April 2007.

27 Qudssia Akhlaque, "India opposes China's entry into SAARC," *Dawn*, 12 November 2005.
28 Rajat Pandit, "India, Nepal Lock Horns Over China's Inclusion," *Times of India*, 13 November 2005.
29 "Afghanistan's Entry Okayed" *Times of India*, 14 November 2005.
30 Ministry of Foreign Affairs of Japan, "The South Asian Association for Regional Cooperation (SAARC) and Japan." Available at: www.mofa.go.jp
31 Ministry of Foreign Affairs of Japan, "The South Asian Association for Regional Cooperation (SAARC) and Japan."
32 Department of Foreign Affairs and Trade, Australia, "Australia invited as observer to the South Asian Association for Regional Cooperation (SAARC) summit." Available at: www.foreignminister.gov.au/releases/2008/fa-s125_08.html.
33 Rashid Ahmad Khan, "The Role of Observers in SAARC," *IPRI Journal* 9, no. 2 (2009): 2.
34 Khan, "The Role of Observers in SAARC," 16.
35 Speech by President Jiang Zemin of the People's Republic of China at Islamabad, Pakistan, 2 December 1996. Text of the full speech available at: www.fmprc.gov.cn/eng/wjdt/zyjh/t24909.htm.
36 See, for instance, the joint communiqué between China and Sri Lanka's foreign ministers, issued on 29 December 2004.
37 "Foreign Ministry Spokesman Qin Gang's Regular Press Conference on March 27, 2007," available at: www.mfa.gov.cn/eng/xwfw/s2510/2511/t306984.htm
38 Su Qiang, "China Makes First Visit to SAARC," *China Daily*, 3 April 2007.
39 "Hu Jintao Meets with Foreign Leaders to the Opening Ceremony of the Beijing Olympic Games." Full text of the remarks available at: www.fmprc.gov.cn/eng/wjb/zzjg/dozys/gjlb/3140/3142/t483123.htm
40 He Hailin, "China and South Asia in a New Perspective," Institute of Asia Pacific Studies, Chinese Academy of Social Sciences (2008). Available at: iaps.cass.cn/english/articles/showcontent.asp?id=1118.
41 For a detailed examination of China's relations with South Asia, see Lawrence Sáez and Crystal Chang, "China and South Asia: Strategic Implications and Economic Imperatives," in *China, the Developing World, and the New Global Dynamic*, eds. Lowell Dittmer and George Yu (Boulder, Col.: Lynne Rienner, 2010), 83–108. Also see Rollie Lal, "China's Relations With South Asia," in *China and the Developing World: Beijing's Strategy for the Twenty-First Century*, eds. Joshua Eisenman, Eric Heginbotham, and Derek Mitchell (Armonk, New York: M. E. Sharpe, 2007), 133–49.
42 Sáez and Chang, "China and South Asia: Strategic Implications and Economic Imperatives," 97.
43 Zhang Yunlin, "China's Economic Progress and its Role in Strengthening Cooperation between East and South Asia," Institute of Asia Pacific Studies, Chinese Academy of Social Sciences (2007). Available at: http://iaps.cass.cn/english/articles/showcontent.asp?id=1126.
44 Zhang Yunlin suggests that a more fruitful avenue for Chinese collaboration with South Asia could be achieved under the framework of the Bangkok Agreement initiated by UNESCAP in 1975. In 2005, this preferential trading arrangement was later renamed the Asia Pacific Trade Agreement. It currently comprises six members (Bangladesh, China, India, Laos, South Korea, and Sri Lanka).

45 Lu Jianren, "The Global Development of Regional Economic Integration," Institute of Asia Pacific Studies, Chinese Academy of Social Sciences (2006). Available at: http://iaps.cass.cn/english/articles/showcontent.asp?id=803&key=SAARC.
46 "Australia and Myanmar to Admit as SAARC Observers," *Colombo Page*, 30 July 2008. Also see "Myanmar Seeks SAARC Membership," *Daily News*, 21 May 2008.
47 Nilofar Suhrawardy, "Iran Considering to Join SAARC, Says Kharazzi," *Arab News* (Jeddah), 23 February 2005.
48 "Iran-SAARC Ties Rooted in History, FM," *Tehran Times*, 1 May 2010.
49 "Agenda to Add China and Iran in SAARC Dropped," E-kantipur.com, 20 April 2010. Available at: www.ekantipur.com/2010/04/20/top-story/agenda-to-add-china-and-iran-in-saarc-dropped/312738/.
50 "India Blocks China SAARC Membership," 2point6billion.com (27 April 2010). Available at: www.2point6billion.com/news/2010/04/27/india-blocks-china-saarc-membership-5479.html.
51 SAARC summit declaration, issued on 2–3 August 2008.
52 For further reference, see Richard Jolly, *UNICEF (United Nations Children's Fund)* (London: Routledge, 2010), and Ian Taylor, *United Nations Conference on Trade and Development (UNCTAD)* (London: Routledge, 2007).
53 At the time of the signing of the MoU, UNODC was known by a different acronym, the United Nations Drug Control Program (UNDCP). For further reference about UNESCO, see J. P. Singh, *United Nations Educational, Scientific and Cultural Organization (UNESCO): Creating Norms for a Complex World* (London: Routledge, 2010).
54 For further reference, see Kelley Lee, *The World Health Organization* (London: Routledge, 2009), Katherine Marshall, *The World Bank: From Reconstruction to Development to Equity* (London: Routledge, 2008), John Shaw, *Global Food and Agricultural Institutions* (London: Routledge, 2009).
55 There is some evidence of joint collaboration projects, mostly resulting in workshops and meetings. See, for instance, *Poverty Reduction in South Asia: Promoting Participation by the Poor: Summary of an Informal Workshop Co-Sponsored by the World Bank and SAARC* (Washington, DC: The World Bank, 1994).
56 "The EU and South Asian Association for Regional Cooperation (SAARC)." Full text available at: http://ec.europa.eu/external_relations/saarc/index_en.htm.
57 Rajendra Jain, "The European Union and Regional Cooperation in South Asia," in *EU-India Relations: A Critique*, ed. Shazia Aziz Wülbers (New Delhi, India: Academic Foundation, 2008), 84.
58 Christopher Piening, *Global Europe: The European Commission in World Affairs* (Boulder, Col.: Lynne Rienner, 1997), 162.
59 Alexander Wendt, *Social Theory of International Politics* (Cambridge: Cambridge University Press, 1999), 186–7.
60 Wendt, "Anarchy is What States Make of It": 391.
61 Wendt, *Social Theory of International Politics*, 317.
62 Morten Bøås, Marianne Marchand, and Timothy Shaw, "The Weave World: The Regional Interweaving of Economies, Ideas and Identities," in *Theories of New Regionalism*, eds. Fredrik Söderbaum and Timothy Shaw (Basingstoke: Palgrave Macmillan, 2003), 197–210.

63 Björn Hettne, "The New Regionalism Revisited," in *Theories of New Regionalism*, eds. Fredrik Söderbaum and Timothy Shaw (Basingstoke: Palgrave Macmillan, 2003), 29. For a similar framework of analysis, also see Iver Neumann, "A Region-Building Approach," in *Theories of New Regionalism*, eds. Fredrik Söderbaum and Timothy Shaw (Basingstoke: Palgrave Macmillan, 2003), 160–78.
64 Barry Buzan, "A Framework for Regional Security Analysis," in *South Asian Insecurity and the Great Powers*, eds. Barry Buzan and Gowher Rizvi (London: Macmillan, 1986), 7.
65 Buzan, "A Framework for Regional Security Analysis," 8.
66 Barry Buzan and Gowher Rizvi, "The Future of the South Asian Security Complex," in *South Asian Insecurity and the Great Powers*, eds. Buzan and Rizvi, 238.
67 Buzan and Rizvi, "The Future of the South Asian Security Complex," 239.
68 Singh, "Framing 'South Asia': Whose Imagined Region?" 6.
69 Buzan and Rizvi, "The Future of the South Asian Security Complex," 245.
70 Buzan, "A Framework for Regional Security Analysis," 11.
71 Buzan, "A Framework for Regional Security Analysis," 11.
72 Barry Buzan, "South Asia Moving Towards Transformation: Emergence of India as a Great Power," *International Studies* 39, no. 1 (2002): 16.
73 Singh, "Framing 'South Asia': Whose Imagined Region?" 8.
74 See, for instance, Mark Beeson, *Institutions of the Asia-Pacific: ASEAN, APEC and Beyond* (London: Routledge, 2009).

**3 Security and economic cooperation**

1 Kishore Dash, "The Political Economy of Regional Cooperation in South Asia," *Pacific Affairs* 69, no. 2 (1996): 185.
2 Dash, "The Political Economy of Regional Cooperation in South Asia": 185.
3 S. D. Muni, "SARC: Building Regionalism From Below," *Asian Survey* 25, no. 4 (1985): 392.
4 Giulio Gallarotti, "The Limits of International Organization: Systematic Failure in the Mismanagement of International Relations," *International Organization* 45, no. 2 (1991): 192–3.
5 John Mearsheimer, "The False Promise of International Institutions," *International Security* 19, No. 3 (1994/1995): 7.
6 Mearsheimer, "The False Promise of International Institutions," 13.
7 Joseph Grieco, "State Interests and Institutional Rule Trajectories: A Neorealist Interpretation of the Maastricht Treaty and European Economic and Monetary Union," *Security Studies* 5, no. 3 (1996): 261–306.
8 Grieco, "State Interests and Institutional Rule Trajectories," 287.
9 Andrew Moravcsik, "Taking Preferences Seriously: A Liberal Theory of International Politics," *International Organization* 51, no. 4 (1997): 513–53.
10 Robert Keohane, "International Institutions: Two Approaches," *International Studies Quarterly* 32, no. 4 (1988): 379–96. Also see Stephan Haggard and Beth Simmons, *International Organization* 41, no. 3 (1987): 491–517.
11 Ernst Haas, *The Uniting of Europe* (Stanford: Stanford University Press, 1958): 10.
12 Ernst Haas, "The Study of Regional Integration: Reflections on the Joy and Anguish of Pretheorizing," in *Regional Integration: Theory and Research*,

eds. Leon Lindberg and Stuart Scheingold (Cambridge, Mass.: Harvard University Press, 1971), 13.

13 Werner Feld and Gavin Boyd, "The Comparative Study of International Regions," in *Comparative Regional Systems*, eds. Werner Feld and Gavin Boyd (New York: Pergamon Press, 1980), 4.

14 Ernst Haas, *The Obsolescence of Regional Integration Theory* (Berkeley, Calif.: Institute of International Studies, 1975).

15 Muni, "SARC: Building Regionalism From Below," 393.

16 Iftekharuzzaman, *The SAARC in Progress: A Hesitant Course of South Asian Transition*. BIISS paper no. 7 (Dhaka: Bangladesh Institute of International and Strategic Studies, 1988), 6.

17 Muhammed Shamshul Huq, "The SARC: Evolution," *Bangladesh Times*, 7 December 1985.

18 Govind Agrawal, "SARC: Quest for a New Political and Economic Order," in *Cooperation Among South Asian Nations*, ed. M. D. Dharamdasani (Varanasi, India: Shalimar Publishing House, 1988), 63.

19 Jimmy Carter, State of the Union Address, 23 January 1980, *Public Papers of the Presidents of the United States: Jimmy Carter, 1976–1984, Book I: 1980–1981* (Washington, DC: Government Printing Office, 1980), 198.

20 Jimmy Carter, State of the Union Address, 23 January 1980, 198.

21 Muni, "SARC: Building Regionalism From Below," 394.

22 Thomas Thornton, "U.S. Strategic Interests in South Asia," in *Dilemmas of National Security Cooperation in India and Pakistan*, ed. Hafeez Malik (New York: St. Martin's Press, 1993), 41.

23 Kail Ellis, "Pakistan's Foreign Policy: Alternating Approaches," in *Dilemmas of National Security Cooperation in India and Pakistan*, ed. Hafeez Malik (New York: St. Martin's Press, 1993), 142.

24 Muni, "SARC: Building Regionalism From Below," 397.

25 Barry Buzan, "South Asia Moving Towards Transformation: Emergence of India as a Great Power," *International Studies* 39, no. 1 (2002): 3.

26 Buzan, "South Asia Moving Towards Transformation," 23.

27 Subrata Mitra, "The Reluctant Hegemon: India's Self-Perception and the South Asian Strategic Environment," *Contemporary South Asia* 12, no. 3 (2003): 399.

28 The sole exception to this claim would be Sri Lanka which, in 1995, had a ratio of military expenditures relative to GDP of 5.9, higher than Pakistan's ratio of 5.3. With the apparent conclusion of the civil war in Sri Lanka, however, it is likely that the country's ratio of military expenditures as a proportion of GDP will decline in future years.

29 Lawrence Sáez, "The Political Economy of the India-Pakistan Nuclear Standoff," in *South Asia's Nuclear Security Dilemma*, ed. Lowell Dittmer (Armonk, New York: M. E. Sharpe, 2005), 3–28.

30 Kishore Dash, "The Political Economy of Regional Cooperation in South Asia," *Pacific Affairs* 69, no. 2 (1996): 188–9.

31 *SAARC Vision Beyond the Year 2000: Report of the SAARC Group of Eminent Persons Established by the Ninth SAARC Summit* (New Delhi, India: Shipra Publications, 1999), xiii.

32 SAARC Convention on Suppression of Terrorism, Article 6.

33 Ministry of Home Affairs, Government of India, *Annual Report 2009–2010* (New Delhi: Ministry of Home Affairs, 2010), 30.

34 Vandana Asthana, *Cross-Border Terrorism in India: Counterterrorism Strategies and Challenges*. Arms Control, Disarmament, and International Security (ACDIS) Occasional Paper, June 2010, 3.
35 Sumit Ganguly, *Counterterrorism Cooperation in South Asia: History and Prospects*. NBR Special Report no. 21, December 2009, 4.
36 SAARC Standing Committee, Twenty-Eight Session, Kathmandu 19–20 August 2002 (SAARC document SAARC/CM.23/SC.28/5), 285.
37 Other SAARC member states had existing domestic legislation to this effect or amended existing legislation to give effect to the principal obligations of the 1987 SAARC convention on suppression of terrorism.
38 For instance, India was unsuccessful in its extradition requests for the November 2008 attacks in Mumbai.
39 SAARC Convention on Suppression of Terrorism, Article 7.
40 Additional Protocol to the SAARC Regional Convention on Suppression of Terrorism, Article 7.
41 Asthana, *Cross-Border Terrorism in India*, 17.
42 Ganguly, *Counterterrorism Cooperation in South Asia*, 8.
43 Edward Mansfield and Helen Milner, "The New Wave of Regionalism," *International Organization* 53, no. 3 (1999): 57.
44 In contrast, India's global imports in 2005 were US $139 billion.
45 Lawrence Sáez, "Trade and Conflict Reduction: Implications for Regional Strategic Stability," *British Journal of Politics and International Relations* 10, no. 4 (2008): 698–716. For a similar argument, also see Saman Kelegama, "SAPTA and its Future," in *The Dynamics of South Asia: Regional Cooperation and SAARC*, eds. Eric Gonsalves and Nancy Jetley (New Delhi, India: Sage Publications, 1999), 175.
46 M. H. Syed, *SAARC: Challenges Ahead* (New Delhi: Kilaso Books, 2003), 55.
47 The Declaration of the Heads of State or Government of the Member Countries of South Asian Association for Regional Cooperation issued on 21 December 1991.
48 These two EPZs are now the largest in the country.
49 Syed, *SAARC: Challenges Ahead*, 43.
50 Indra Nath Mukherji, "SAFTA: Addressing the Unfinished Agenda," in *SAARC: The Road Ahead*, eds. Iqbal Ahmed Saradgi, S. K. Sahni, and R. N. Srivastava (New Delhi, India: Foundation for Peace and Sustainable Development, 2007), 85.
51 Indra Nath Mukherji, "Charting a Free Trade Area in South Asia: Instruments and Modalities," in *Trade, Finance, and Investment in South Asia*, ed. T. N. Srinivasan (New Delhi, India: Social Science Press, 2002), 98.
52 The Declaration of the Ninth SAARC Summit of the Heads of State or Government of the Member Countries of the South Asian Association for Regional Cooperation issued on 14 May 1997, in Malé, Maldives.
53 The Declaration of the Tenth SAARC Summit of the Heads of State or Government of the Member Countries of the South Asian Association for Regional Cooperation issued on 31 July 1998, in Colombo, Sri Lanka.
54 Agreement on South Asian Free Trade Area (SAFTA), Article 4.
55 Agreement for Establishment of SAARC Arbitration Council, Article 2.
56 SAARC Limited Multilateral Agreement on Avoidance of Double Taxation and Mutual Administrative Assistance in Tax Matters, Articles 5 and 6.

57 SAARC Limited Multilateral Agreement on Avoidance of Double Taxation and Mutual Administrative Assistance in Tax Matters, Article 3.
58 Agreement on the Establishment of South Asian Regional Standards Organisation (SARSO), Preamble.
59 For further reference on the ISO and similar institutions, see Craig Murphy and JoAnne Yates, *The International Organization for Standardization and the Global Economy* (London: Routledge, 2009).
60 Agreement on the Establishment of South Asian Regional Standards Organisation (SARSO), Article 3.
61 The figures show percentage increases or decreases in imports and exports by a single country with the rest of South Asia. I have indexed import and export levels with other SAARC members whereby 2004 = 100. Please note that the IMF's *Direction of Trade Statistics* does not maintain trade data for Bhutan.

**4 The dimensions of regional collaboration in South Asia**

1 The World Bank's poverty headcount ratio represents the percentage of the population living on US $1.25 a day (calculated at purchasing power parity or PPP). Macrolevel World Bank developmental data is available at the World Bank's International Development Association (IDA) website: www.worldbank.org/ida. For the sake of contrast over time, South Asia's poverty headcount ratio in 1990 is equivalent to sub-Saharan Africa's poverty headcount ratio in 2005.
2 Net per capita IDA assistance to South Asian countries declined slightly from 1990 to 2000, but increased consistently from 2001 onwards.
3 Ernst Haas, *The Uniting of Europe: Political, Social, and Economic Forces, 1950–1957* (Stanford, Calif.: Stanford University Press, 1958), xv–xvi.
4 Joseph Nye, "Comparative Regional Integration: Concept and Measurement," *International Organization* 22, no. 4 (1968): 858–75.
5 "SARC Meet for Better Future: PM," *Hindustan Times*, 6 December 1985.
6 Syed Zillur Rahman, "SARC to Provide Scope for Dialogue," *Bangladesh Observer*, 6 December 1985.
7 Rahman, "SARC to Provide Scope for Dialogue."
8 "Zia Sees Domination by India," *Hindustan Times*, 8 December 1985. President Zia's misquote was also discussed in an editorial in the same newspaper. See "Zia's Dilemma in Dhaka," *Hindustan Times*, 8 December 1985.
9 "Everyone in SAARC is Equal: PM," *The Statesman*, 10 December 1985.
10 Faruq Choudhury, "Evolution of SARC," *Bangladesh Observer*, 7 December 1985.
11 Choudhury, "Evolution of SARC."
12 Syedur Rahman, "Issues and Agenda for South Asia Regional Cooperation: A Bangladeshi Perspective," *Asian Survey* 25, no. 4 (April 1985): 411. He later contends that smaller countries have engaged in international relationships as a form of "blanket of protection" to counteract domination by India.
13 "A Paper on the Proposal for Regional Cooperation in South Asia," *Milestones in the Evolution of Regional Cooperation in South Asia (1980–1988), Volume I* (Kathmandu, Nepal: SAARC Secretariat), 3–6.
14 Joint Communiqué Issued at the Conclusion of First Meeting of Foreign Secretaries, Colombo April 21–23, 1981. *From SARC to SAARC: Milestones*

*in the Evolution of Regional Cooperation in South Asia (1980–1988), Volume I* (Kathmandu: SAARC Secretariat, 1988), 9–10.

15 "It is Time for Formalised Regional Co-Operation," *Ceylon Daily News*, 22 April 1981.

16 Umashanker Phadnis, "Colombo Accord on Co-Operation," *Hindustan Times*, 24 April 1981.

17 A. S. Abraham, "Co-operation in South Asia: Seven States in Search of a Link," *Times of India*, 24 April 1981.

18 Neville de Silva, "Toward Regional Co-operation," *Ceylon Daily News*, 22 April 1981.

19 Sumit Ganguly, "The Prospects for SAARC," in *Dilemmas of National Security Cooperation in India and Pakistan*, ed. Hafeez Malik (New York: St. Martin's Press, 1993), 279–80.

20 A useful descriptive narrative about the development of SAARC's integrated plan of action can be found in Mahendra P. Lama, "SAARC Integrated Plan of Action: Towards More Effective Cooperation," *South Asian Survey* 5, no. 1 (1998): 39–56.

21 K. Nadarajah, "Committee Identifies Action for South Asian Seven," *Daily News*, 11 January 1983.

22 "SARC Formulates Program of Action," *Daily News*, 14 January 1983.

23 The full text of the declaration can be found in "7 Asian Nations Resolve to Step Up Co-Operation," *Hindustan Times*, 3 August 1983. Also see "Foreign Ministers Sign Joint Plan of Action," *The Statesman*, 3 August 1983.

24 Mishra, *Dhaka Summit and SAARC*, 15.

25 Mishra, *Dhaka Summit and SAARC*, 15.

26 Prior to its inception, several names had been proposed for a South Asian regional forum. In its initial working draft for the creation of a South Asian regional forum, other proposed names included: South Asian Association for Cooperation (SAAC), Association of South Asia (ASA), Association of South Asia for Cooperation (ASAC), and Organisation of South Asian States (OSAS). See Ghulam Umar, *SAARC: Analytical Survey* (Karachi: Pakistan Institute of International Affairs, 1988), 142–3. Also see Pramod Kumar Mishra, "Regional Cooperation in South Asia: Constraints and Realities," in *Cooperation Among South Asian Nations*, ed. M. D. Dharamdasani (Varanasi, India: Shalimar Publishing House, 1988), 167.

27 Muhammed Shamshul Huq, "The SARC: Evolution," *Bangladesh Times*, 7 December 1985.

28 Huq, "The SARC: Evolution."

29 Huq, "The SARC: Evolution."

30 Iqbal Sobhan Chowdhury, "SARC Declaration Drafting Body Set Up," *Bangladesh Observer*, 4 December 1985.

31 "SARC Charter Endorsed, Draft Declaration Okayed," *Bangladesh Observer*, 5 December 1985.

32 A detailed narrative about the ingredients of the IPA can be found in M. H. Syed, *SAARC: Challenges Ahead* (New Delhi, India: Kilaso Books, 2003), 16–36.

33 See O. P. Goel, *India and SAARC Engagements*, Vol. 1 (Delhi, India: Isha Books, 2004), 7–18.

34 Mahendra P. Lama, *Integrated Programme of Action in SAARC: Genesis, Evaluation, Constraints, and Rationale for Revamping* (New Delhi, India:

Research and Information System for the Non-Aligned and Other Developing Countries, 1999), 416.

35 Dhaka Declaration of the Heads of State or Government of the Member States of South Asian Association for Regional Cooperation, 7–8 December 1985.

36 Social Charter of the South Asian Association for Regional Cooperation, Article 1.

37 Dhaka Declaration of the Heads of State or Government of the Member States of South Asian Association for Regional Cooperation, 12–13 November 2005, clause 11.

38 Thimpu Declaration of the Heads of State or Government of the Member States of South Asian Association for Regional Cooperation, 28–29 April 2010, clause 19.

39 There are no literacy data for Bhutan until 2005. No data for Afghanistan are available for this period. Nonetheless, Afghanistan was not a member of SAARC at the time of the fourth SAARC summit.

40 According to the latest available population estimates, in 2010 over 64 percent of the population in Afghanistan was under 25 years of age. The figures for youth population in Nepal and Pakistan exceeded 57 percent, while in Bangladesh (53 percent) and Bhutan (51 percent) the majority of the population was under 25 years of age. Over 48 percent of the population of India and the Maldives was also under 25 years of age. The sole demographic exception in South Asia is Sri Lanka, where only 39 percent of the population was under 25 years of age. Data on population has been gathered from the U.S. Census Bureau, International Data Base (IDB), available at: www.census.gov/ipc/www/idb/groups.php.

41 To illustrate this point, according to the latest available data from the 1998 census in Pakistan, the overall female literacy rate in Pakistan is 32.02 percent, but the rural literacy rate for females is 20.09 percent. Interregional disparities are also quite stark. For instance, the overall female literacy rate in the provinces of the North-West Frontier Province and Balochistan are 18.82 and 14.09 percent, respectively. The rural female literacy rates in these two provinces are 14.69 and 7.94 percent, respectively. See Statistics Division, Federal Bureau of Statistics, Government of Pakistan, *Statistical Year Book 2009* (Islamabad, Pakistan: Federal Bureau of Statistics), 330.

42 For a comparative perspective, one should look at public expenditure on education in Japan and Singapore, two Asian countries with a strong record of educational achievement. In the 1990s, Japan spent the equivalent of about 3.5 percent of GDP on education; Singapore spent about 3.1 percent.

43 Joint Communiqué, Ministerial Meeting on Women in Development, Shillong, India, issued on 8 May 1986.

44 Bangalore Declaration of the Heads of State or Government of the Member States of South Asian Association for Regional Cooperation, 16–17 November 1986, clause 10.

45 M. H. Syed, *SAARC: Challenges Ahead* (New Delhi, India: Kilaso Books, 2003), 30.

46 At a symbolic level, SAARC has designated 2010 as the Year Against Gender Based Violence. Readers may wish to learn more about SGIB by looking at its website available at: www.genderinfobase.org.

47 For earlier scholarly work on the relationship between educational attainment and income levels, please see Jacob Mincer, "The Distribution of Labor Incomes: A Survey With Special Reference to the Human Capital Approach," *Journal of Economic Literature* 8, no. 1 (1970): 1–26; and Jacob Mincer, *Schooling Experience and Earnings* (New York: NBER, 1974). A large body of recent literature has drawn attention to the relationship between educational attainment, inequality, and economic growth. See, for instance, Jess Benhabib, and Mark Spiegel, "The Role of Human Capital in Economic Development: Evidence from Aggregate Cross-Country Data," *Journal of Monetary Economics* 34, no. 2 (1994): 143–74; Robert Barro, "Human Capital and Growth," *American Economic Review* 91, no. 2 (2001): 12–17; Erik Hanushek and Ludger Woessmann, *The Role of Education Quality for Economic Growth*, World Bank Policy Research Working Paper No. 4122 (1 February 2007).

48 Dhaka Declaration of the Heads of State or Government of the Member States of South Asian Association for Regional Cooperation, 12–13 November 2005.

49 During interviews at the SAARC Secretariat, I was informed that further developments on Manmohan Singh's proposal had bypassed the standard protocol for incorporating items into the SAARC summit agenda. In this particular case, for instance, the matter was referred directly to the SAARC Standing Committee for follow-up action to take place.

50 New Delhi Declaration of the Heads of State or Government of the Member States of South Asian Association for Regional Cooperation, 3–4 April 2007.

51 Prior to the changes exempting Pakistani staff and students of the South Asian University from the visa regime, Pakistani nationals are expected to register with the police and face severe travel restrictions that limited them to only visit three cities in India. Indian nationals visiting Pakistan face a reciprocal arrangement.

52 During interviews with individuals who were engaged in the inter-governmental steering committee in charge of directing and implementing the administrative arrangements for the establishment of the university, it was repeatedly noted that Indian and Pakistani delegations were able to iron out differences quite effectively. Some interviewees noted, though, that the greater difficulties in implementing the establishment of the university came from delegations from smaller countries.

53 See Syed, *SAARC: Challenges Ahead*, 36–38. Also see Goel, *India and SAARC Engagements*, 18–23.

54 SAARC Vision Beyond the Year 2000: Report of the SAARC Group of Eminent Persons Established by the Ninth SAARC Summit (New Delhi, India: Shipra Publications, 1999), xiii.

55 Goel, *India and SAARC Engagements*, 66–71.

56 I.H. Zaki, "SAARC: Beyond the First Decade," *South Asian Survey* 3, no. 1–2 (1996): 61.

**5 Future challenges**

1 A similar evaluative approach is undertaken by Q. K. Ahmad, "SAARC: Envisioning the Future," *South Asian Survey* 9, no. 2 (2002): 187–99.

2 Joseph Nye, "Comparative Regional Integration: Concept and Measurement," *International Organization* 22, no. 4 (1968): 858–75.
3 Foreign Policy and the Fund for Peace, *2010 Failed States Index*. Data available at: www.foreignpolicy.com/articles/2010/06/21/2010_failed_states_index_interactive_map_and_rankings. In 2010, the five countries with a worse failed states index score were Somalia, Chad, Sudan, Zimbabwe, and the Democratic Republic of the Congo.
4 SAARC Charter, Article 10.1.
5 SAARC Charter, Article 9.1.
6 Foreign Policy and the Fund for Peace, *2009 Failed States Index*. Data available at: www.foreignpolicy.com/articles/2010/06/21/2010_failed_states_index_interactive_map_and_rankings.
7 Constitutive Act of the African Union, Article 30.
8 Constitutive Act of the African Union, Article 23.
9 The original Constitutive Act of the African Union contained an article (Article 31) which enabled the Union to expel a member. This article, however, was deleted in Article 12 of the Protocol on Amendments to the Constitutive Act of the African Union.
10 Prime Minister's Office, Government of India, "PMs IDSA Anniversary Speech," 11 November 2005. The full text of the speech is available at: http://pmindia.nic.in/speech/content.asp?id=218
11 Noor ul Haq, "The Future of SAARC Hinges on Kashmir," *Dawn*, 10 December 2005.
12 Government of the Maldives, National Environment Action Plan, *Second National Environmental Action Plan* (Malé, Maldives: Ministry of Home Affairs, Housing and Environment, 1999).
13 See Intergovernmental Panel on Climate Change, *IPPC Third Assessment Report* (Geneva: IPCC Secretariat, 2001), especially Chapters 11 and 17.
14 For reports that are skeptical about the projection that the Maldives is under threat, see Nils-Axel Mörner, Michael Tooley, and Göran Possnert, "New Perspectives for the Future of the Maldives," *Global and Planetary Change* 40, no. 1–2 (2004): 177–82; and Nils-Axel Mörner, "The Maldives Project: A Future Free from Sea-Level," *Contemporary South Asia* 13, no. 2 (2004): 149–55.
15 President's Office, Government of the Maldives, *Aneh Dhivehi Raajje: The Strategic Action Plan. National Framework for Development 2009–2013* (Malé, Maldives: President's Office, 2009), 390.
16 President's Office, Government of the Maldives, *Aneh Dhivehi Raajje: The Strategic Action Plan*, 390.
17 See T. V. Paul, ed., *South Asia's Weak States: Understanding the Regional Insecurity Predicament* (Palo Alto, Calif.: Stanford University Press, 2010).
18 Hafeez Malik, "Dilemmas of National Security Cooperation," in *Dilemmas of National Security Cooperation in India and Pakistan*, ed. Hafeez Malik (New York: St. Martin's Press, 1993), 3.
19 Dash, *Regionalism in South Asia: Negotiating Cooperation, Institutional Structures* (London: Routledge, 2008), 96.
20 Dash, *Regionalism in South Asia*, 96.
21 The CTBT is an arms control treaty that prohibits all nuclear test explosions. The CTBT was open to signing starting in September 1996. Article XIV of the CTBT specifies that the treaty will come into force 180 days

after the ratification by all states listed in Annex 2 of the treaty. Annex 2 of the CTBT lists 44 countries which formally participated in the work of the 1996 session of the Conference on Disarmament. Three of these named countries listed in Annex 2 (India, Pakistan, and North Korea) have not yet signed the CTBT. Six other named states (China, Egypt, Indonesia, Iran, Israel, and the United States) have signed, but not ratified, the CTBT.

22 Seminal theoretical work on the security dilemma can be traced to John Herz, *Political Realism and Political Idealism* (Chicago: University of Chicago Press, 1951). Contemporary understandings of the security dilemma include Robert Jervis, "Cooperation under the Security Dilemma," *World Politics* 30, no. 2 (1978): 167–74; and Robert Jervis, *Perception and Misperception in International Politics* (Princeton, NJ: Princeton University Press, 1978), 58–113. The application of the security dilemma to South Asia is most identified with the work of Sumit Ganguly, "Explaining the Kashmir Insurgency: Political Mobilization and Institutional Decay," *International Security* 21, no. 2 (1996): 76–107.

23 William Rose, "The Security Dilemma and Ethnic Conflict: Some New Hypotheses," *Security Studies* 9, no. 4 (2000): 3.

24 Rose, "The Security Dilemma and Ethnic Conflict: Some New Hypotheses," 3.

25 Given the sensitivity regarding the terminology used to describe the conflict over Kashmir, I consider the acronyms used in this section (i.e., IAK, PAK, LOC) to be the most neutral. However, in other sources, readers are also likely to see references to Indian-occupied Kashmir (IOK) and Pakistan-occupied Kashmir (POK). The Pakistani government formally refers to the PAK as Azaad Jammu o-Kashmir (AJK) or Azaad Kashmir (Free Kashmir).

26 Lowell Dittmer, "Introduction: South Asia's Nuclear Security Dilemma," in *South Asia's Nuclear Security Dilemma*, ed. Lowell Dittmer (Armonk, NY: M. E. Sharpe, 2005), vii–xi.

27 The NNPT is a multilateral treaty that encompasses a broad range of coverage on the issues of nuclear non-proliferation, disarmament, and the peaceful use of nuclear energy. The NNPT took effect on 5 March 1970. India and Pakistan, together with Israel, are not signatories to the NNPT.

28 The Declaration of the Tenth SAARC Summit of the Heads of State or Government of the Member Countries of the South Asian Association for Regional Cooperation issued on 31 July 1998, in Colombo, Sri Lanka.

29 The Declaration of the Tenth SAARC Summit, 31 July 1998.

30 For a comparison, see clause 78 of the 10th SAARC summit declaration and clause 31 of the 11th SAARC summit declaration.

31 The removal of the clauses referring to nuclear non-proliferation and nuclear disarmament appears to be deliberate since reference to these issues has appeared uniformly in every single SAARC summit declaration starting from the 1st SAARC summit declaration.

32 The Declaration of the Twelfth SAARC Summit of the Heads of State or Government of the Member Countries of the South Asian Association for Regional Cooperation issued on 6 January 2004, in Islamabad, Pakistan.

33 The Declaration of the Twelfth SAARC Summit, 6 January 2004.

34 Confidence-building measures are designed to reduce tensions and to promote positive relations between adversaries. They include a range of communication, constraint, transparency, and verification procedures. The seminal theoretical work on confidence-building measures, as currently understood,

is by Johan Jørgen Holst, "Confidence Building Measures: A Conceptual Framework," *Survival 25*, no.1 (1983): 2–15. A useful illustration of the application of CBMs in a South Asian context can be seen in Ross Masood, *Towards a New Regional Order in South Asia* (Delhi, India: Media House, 2004), 74–113. Also see chapters by Christian Wagner, S. D. Muni, and Pervaiz Iqbal Cheema in Mohammed Humanyun Kabir, ed., *Confidence Building Measures and Security Cooperation in South Asia: Challenges in the New Century* (Dhaka, Bangladesh: Academic Press, 2002).

35 Memorandum of Understanding signed by the foreign secretary of India, K. Raghunath, and the foreign secretary of Pakistan, Shamshad Ahmad, in Lahore on 21 February 1999.

36 Lahore declaration signed by the prime ministers of India and Pakistan on 21 February 1999.

37 See, for instance, Charles Kupchan, *How Enemies Become Friends: The Sources of Stable Peace* (Princeton, NJ: Princeton University Press, 2010).

38 Sumit Ganguly and Kent Biringer, "Nuclear Crisis Stability in South Asia," in *South Asia's Nuclear Security Dilemma*, ed. Lowell Dittmer (Armonk: NY: M. E. Sharpe, 2005), 29–48.

39 The other elements of the composite dialogue between India and Pakistan include: broad collaboration on peace and security, dialogue on the resolution of the Jammu and Kashmir dispute, joint collaboration on the Wullar Barrage/Tulbul navigation project, provisions for joint redeployment in the Siachen Glacier, joint survey of barrage pillars along the Sir Creek estuary, cooperation on terrorism and drug trafficking, and economic and commercial cooperation.

40 Masood, *Towards a New Regional Order in South Asia*, 61.

41 S. Akbar Zaidi, "Economic CBMs in South Asia: Trade as a Precursor to Peace With India," in *The Challenge of Confidence-Building Measures in South Asia*, ed. Moonis Ahmar (New Delhi, India: Har-Anand Publications, 2001): 332.

42 Rahman, "Issues and Agenda for South Asia Regional Cooperation," 413.

43 Lawrence Sáez, "Trade and Conflict Reduction: Implications for Regional Strategic Stability," *British Journal of Politics and International Relations* 10, no. 4 (2008): 698–716.

44 The data in Table 5.1 are derived from the World Bank's definition of services. In that definition, services correspond to the classification provided by International Standard Industrial Classification (ISIC). Indicators in the ISIC definition include value added in wholesale and retail trade (including hotels and restaurants), transport, and government, financial, professional, and other forms of personal services (e.g., education, health care, real estate services).

45 Indra Nath Mukherji, "SAFTA: Addressing the Unfinished Agenda," in *SAARC: The Road Ahead*, ed. Iqbal Ahmed Saradgi, S. K. Sahni, and R. N. Srivastava (New Delhi, India: Foundation for Peace and Sustainable Development, 2007), 98.

46 For an overview of these challenges, see Neela Mukherjee, "SAARC Countries, Regional Trade in Services and WTO: Issues and Prospects," *South Asian Survey* 9, no. 2 (2002): 239–49.

47 Bela Balassa, *The Theory of Economic Integration* (Homewood, Ill.: Richard Irwin, 1961), 1.

48 Shrikant Paranjpe, "Development of Order in South Asia: Towards a South Asian Association for Regional Cooperation Parliament," *Contemporary South Asia* 11, no. 3 (2002): 349.
49 Dipankar Bannerjee and N. Manoharan, eds., *SAARC: Towards Greater Connectivity* (New Delhi, India: Konrad Adenauer Stiftung, 2008).
50 Govind Agrawal, "SARC: Quest for a New Political and Economic Order," in *Cooperation Among South Asian Nations*, ed. M. D. Dharamdasani (Varanasi, India: Shalimar Publishing House, 1988), 61.
51 Godfrey Gunatilleke, *Cooperation Among Small Nations in Asia in the Context of the Changing Asian Political Economy* (Colombo, Sri Lanka: Marga Institute, 1979), 4.
52 Agrawal, "SARC: Quest for a New Political and Economic Order," 62.
53 Abul Ahsan, *SAARC: A Perspective* (Dhaka, Bangladesh: University Press Limited, 1992), 19.
54 Ahsan, *SAARC: A Perspective*, 19.
55 This argument was first developed by M. L. Sondhi and Srikant Paranjpe, "SAARC Parliament," *Hindustan Times*, 27 July 1990. A more theoretically-driven proposal is made by Shrikant Paranjpe, "Development of Order in South Asia: Towards a South Asian Association for Regional Cooperation Parliament," 352–4.
56 Nye, "Comparative Regional Integration," 875.
57 Nye, "Comparative Regional Integration," 863.
58 Nephil Matangi Maskay, "Monetary Cooperation in South Asia," *Economic and Political Weekly* 38, no. 51–52 (27 December 2003): 5,341.
59 Albert Fishlow and Stephan Haggard, *The United States and the Regionalisation of the World Economy* (Paris: Organisation for Economic Co-operation and Development, 1992), 13.
60 Sumit Ganguly, "The Prospects for SAARC," in *Dilemmas of National Security Cooperation in India and Pakistan*, ed. Hafeez Malik (New York: St. Martin's Press, 1993), 289.

# Select bibliography

Abul Ahsan, *SAARC: A Perspective* (Dhaka, Bangladesh: University Press Ltd, 1992). Useful selection of documents and intriguing analysis of SAARC from its first secretary general.

Anil Bhuimali and Chandan K. Mukhopadhyay, *Economic Issues in SAARC Context* (Delhi, India: Abhijeet Publications, 2008). Fairly detailed quantitative analysis of the principal macroeconomic issues and trends facing different SAARC members.

Imtiaz Bokhari, S. D. Muni, Syedur Rahman, Sridhar K. Khatri, and Mohammed Ayoob, "SARC: Four Views and a Comparative Perspective (special issue)," *Asian Survey* 25, no. 4 (April 1985). Excellent collection of essays about SAARC by leading academic authorities from the region.

Kishore Dash, *Regionalism in South Asia: Negotiating Cooperation, Institutional Structures* (London: Routledge, 2008). This book excels in providing clear cross-national comparisons and highlighting intraregional complementarities, but sadly only devotes one chapter to SAARC.

Dhirendra Dwivedi, *SAARC: Problems and Prospects* (New Delhi, India: Adhyayan Publishers, 2008). Builds on a similar premise focused on the outcome of summits, in this particular case providing a narrative description of the first 12 SAARC summits.

D. K. Ghosh, *New Frontiers: Pathways for SAARC* (New Delhi, India: Sunrise Publications, 2004). Creditable effort at evaluating the evolution of SAARC economies, though written prior to the time of the signing of the SAFTA.

O. P. Goel, *India and SAARC Engagements* (New Delhi, India: Isha Books, 2004). Exhaustive description about the declarations emerging from the first 10 SAARC summits.

Ranjan Modi, *SAARC: Regional and Global Perspectives* (Jaipur, India: Mangal Deep Publications, 2004). Commendable for its ambition to internationalize the focus on SAARC.

SAARC, *SAARC Vision Beyond the Year 2000: Report of the SAARC Group of Eminent Persons Established by the Ninth SAARC Summit* (New Delhi, India: Shipra Publications, 1999). Uncharacteristically frank and critical assessment of SAARC from a SAARC-sponsored committee.

——, *From SARC to SAARC: Milestones in the Evolution of Regional Cooperation in South Asia (1980–1988), Volume I* (Kathmandu, Nepal: SAARC Secretariat, 1988). This volume, filled with hard-to-obtain SAARC documents, speeches, and declarations, will appeal to scholars who wish to trace the process of regional collaboration leading to the creation of SAARC.

M. H. Syed, *SAARC: Challenges Ahead* (New Delhi, India: Kilaso Books, 2003). Although somewhat descriptive and uncritical, it is a reliable source for information about various SAARC programs and initiatives.

# Index

Italic page numbers indicate tables; bold indicate figures.